The History of Wine

CRAFTED BY SKRIUWER

Copyright © 2025 by Skriuwer.

All rights reserved. No part of this book may be used or reproduced in any form whatsoever without written permission except in the case of brief quotations in critical articles or reviews.

At **Skriuwer**, we're more than just a team—we're a global community of people who love books. In Frisian, "Skriuwer" means "writer," and that's at the heart of what we do: creating and sharing books with readers worldwide. Wherever you are in the world, **Skriuwer** is here to inspire learning.

Frisian is one of the oldest languages in Europe, closely related to English and Dutch, and is spoken by about **500,000 people** in the province of **Friesland** (Fryslân), located in the northern Netherlands. It's the second official language of the Netherlands, but like many minority languages, Frisian faces the challenge of survival in a modern, globalized world.

We're using the money we earn to promote the Frisian language.

For more information, contact : **kontakt@skriuwer.com** (www.skriuwer.com)

Disclaimer:
The images in this book are creative reinterpretations of historical scenes. While every effort was made to accurately capture the essence of the periods depicted, some illustrations may include artistic embellishments or approximations. They are intended to evoke the atmosphere and spirit of the times rather than serve as precise historical records.

TABLE OF CONTENTS

CHAPTER 1: THE EARLIEST TRACES OF WINE

- *Discovery of ancient pottery residues in the Caucasus*
- *Domestication of wild grapevines for early winemaking*
- *Ritual significance of wine in prehistoric communities*

CHAPTER 2: WINE IN ANCIENT EGYPT

- *Egyptian tomb paintings depicting grape harvesting and pressing*
- *Use of wine in royal and funerary ceremonies*
- *Differentiation between beer as a daily drink and wine as a luxury*

CHAPTER 3: THE WORLD OF MESOPOTAMIA & WINE'S GROWTH

- *Trade networks spreading wine across the Fertile Crescent*
- *Religious offerings of wine to Mesopotamian deities*
- *Early written records (cuneiform tablets) referencing wine rations*

CHAPTER 4: WINE IN ANCIENT GREECE

- *Symposia as social and philosophical gatherings*
- *Dionysus as the god of wine and ecstasy*
- *Influence of Greek colonization on vineyard expansion*

CHAPTER 5: THE ROMAN EMPIRE & WINE

- *Widespread viticulture through Roman roads and conquests*
- *Advanced techniques in pressing, storage, and aging*
- *Emergence of famed Roman wines (Falernian, Caecuban) and amphora labeling*

CHAPTER 6: WINE IN EARLY CHRISTIAN & MONASTIC TRADITIONS

- Sacramental wine in the Eucharist and monastic preservation
- Expansion of vineyards around medieval monasteries
- Detailed vineyard records and the concept of vineyard terroir

---

CHAPTER 7: WINE IN THE MEDIEVAL PERIOD

- Feudalism's influence on vineyard ownership and labor
- Church festivals, pilgrimages, and the role of wine in religious life
- Rise of trade fairs and guilds shaping wine distribution

CHAPTER 8: RENAISSANCE EUROPE & THE RISE OF WINE TRADE

- Renewed interest in classical texts on viticulture
- Increased maritime commerce spreading wine across Europe
- Growth of merchant classes and urban demand for refined wines

---

CHAPTER 9: WINE DURING THE AGE OF EXPLORATION

- Introduction of Old World grapes to the Americas, Africa, and Asia
- Fortified wine techniques to survive long sea voyages
- Role of missionaries establishing vineyards in colonial territories

---

CHAPTER 10: WINE IN THE 17TH CENTURY

- Improvements in glass bottle production and cork usage
- Growing English appetite for imported wines (claret, port, sherry)
- Regulations and tavern culture shaping public wine consumption

CHAPTER 11: WINE IN THE 18TH CENTURY

- Methuen Treaty boosting Portuguese wine exports to England
- Increasing middle-class demand for higher-quality wines
- Refined practices of aging, labeling, and blending across Europe

---

CHAPTER 12: COLONIAL WINE PRACTICES

- Spanish missions in the Americas (Mexico, Chile, Argentina)
- Cape Colony's wine culture under Dutch and French Huguenot influence
- Religious and forced-labor systems impacting vineyard development

---

CHAPTER 13: WINE IN THE EARLY 19TH CENTURY

- Aftermath of Napoleonic Wars and shifting trade routes
- Independence movements in Latin America allowing local vineyard growth
- Refinements in bottling, cellar methods, and a nascent scientific approach

---

CHAPTER 14: THE SPREAD OF VINE DISEASES & THEIR IMPACT

- Powdery mildew, downy mildew, and the devastation of phylloxera
- Failed chemical treatments and eventual adoption of grafting
- Replanting vineyards with American rootstocks and evolving wine science

---

CHAPTER 15: WINE IN CULTURAL CEREMONIES AND CELEBRATIONS

- Communal feasts, harvest festivals, and sacral libations
- Religious rites in Judaism (Kiddush) and Christianity (Eucharist)
- Symbolic roles of wine in weddings, funerals, and court banquets

CHAPTER 16: UNDERSTANDING HISTORICAL GRAPE VARIETIES

- Evolution from wild Vitis vinifera to cultivated strains
- Synonyms and local naming leading to confusion in identification
- Influence of phylloxera on preserving and choosing key grape varieties

CHAPTER 17: WINE IN ART & LITERATURE THROUGH HISTORY

- Depictions on ancient pottery (Greek vases) & Roman frescos
- Religious iconography in medieval manuscripts & Renaissance paintings
- Literary themes from Homer to Shakespeare, revealing wine's social depth

CHAPTER 18: NOTABLE HISTORICAL WINE REGIONS (UP TO THE 19TH CENTURY)

- Bordeaux, Burgundy, Champagne, Rhine, Douro, Sherry, Tokaj, and more
- Regional grape specialties & evolving export markets
- Colonial expansions leading to new vineyards in the Americas & beyond

CHAPTER 19: GROWING WINE KNOWLEDGE & TECHNIQUES

- Incremental learning from ancient to early 19th-century cellar practices
- Monastic stewardship, Renaissance curiosity, and early scientific hints
- Formation of merchant networks, blending methods, and improved storage

CHAPTER 20: REFLECTIONS AND THE ROAD TO THE EARLY MODERN ERA

- Summation of wine's cultural, religious, and artistic significance
- Milestones like phylloxera, industrial-era transport, and nascent enology
- Lasting legacies that shaped modern wine's global presence

CHAPTER 1

The Earliest Traces of Wine

Introduction

Wine is one of the oldest alcoholic drinks made by humans. It has a long past that begins in very ancient times, long before people kept written records. Many historians believe that the beginnings of wine happened by accident when wild grapes, crushed by natural events or animals, turned into fermented juice. Once people tasted it and felt its effects, they tried to understand and recreate it.

In this chapter, we will look at the earliest evidence of wine. We will explore how people began to notice that grape juice could turn into an interesting and flavorful beverage. We will also learn about the role of geography, climate, and the simple tools and containers used by early people.

Ancient Beginnings in the Near East and the Caucasus

The Birthplace Theories

There is evidence that the first wines might have been produced in regions near the Caucasus Mountains, in an area that may include parts of present-day Georgia and Armenia. This region is known for its wild grape vines and suitable climate. Some archaeologists discovered very old pottery vessels that show signs of grape seeds, skins, and chemical residues linked to wine. These findings suggest that people in these areas were making wine over 7,000 to 8,000 years ago.

The climate in the Caucasus is varied, with sunny summers and enough rainfall to let grapes grow. Wild grapes are common there, which might have given local people an easy source of fruit. Early winemakers noticed that if they kept grape juice in a container, it could transform into wine.

At the same time, many experts say that it is also possible that other parts of the Fertile Crescent region, such as eastern Turkey or northern Iran, might have discovered wine on their own. Grapes can grow in many different places, so early wine experiments might have taken place in multiple regions. However, the Caucasus region has some of the oldest known tools and pottery associated with wine production.

Early Containers and Methods

Pottery was very important for early wine storage. People learned to shape clay into jars or pots and fire them so they became hard and waterproof. In Georgia, a special type of clay vessel called a "qvevri" has been used for centuries (and still is today, though we are not discussing modern times in depth, just acknowledging the tradition). These large clay vessels were buried underground to keep the temperature steady. Ancient people would crush grapes, pour the juice into these vessels, and allow fermentation to happen naturally.

Early winemakers did not fully understand the science behind yeast and fermentation. They only saw that grapes, left alone in a container, would bubble and turn into an alcoholic drink. Sometimes they might have added wild herbs or other fruits, but mostly it was plain grapes. Over time, these people became skilled at choosing ripe grapes and crushing them in a way that made good wine.

Because these events took place many thousands of years ago, we do not have written descriptions of how it all happened. Instead, we rely on archaeological evidence, chemical tests on pottery shards, and leftover grape seeds and stems. These clues help scientists and historians piece together how early wine might have been made.

The Role of Domestication

Wine did not just appear out of nowhere. Grapes come from wild plants, and over time, humans learned to domesticate these wild vines. Domestication is the process in which people pick plants (or animals) with desirable traits and encourage them to breed or grow. In the case of grapes, early farmers noticed which vines had sweeter grapes, bigger clusters, or made a tastier wine. By replanting cuttings from these vines, they gradually shaped the grapes to have qualities that were good for winemaking.

Domesticated grapes often produced more fruit and had a higher sugar content, which makes fermentation easier. Sugar feeds yeast, and yeast makes alcohol. Early winemakers probably carried cuttings of successful grapevines to new areas, spreading wine culture further.

Ritual and Early Social Meaning

Wine was not just a casual drink. From early on, it had special meaning. People realized that wine can make a person feel relaxed or even dreamy. This likely led some groups to think of wine as a gift from the gods or spirits. Archaeological sites from places like ancient Georgia or Armenia sometimes show that wine-making areas were near places that might have been used for worship. Drinking wine together may have also helped people bond during gatherings or tribal meetings.

The magical process of fermentation, which changed sweet juice into a strong drink, made wine seem even more special. Early myths might have grown around wine's discovery, turning it into a sacred or mystical substance. In some places, people used wine in rituals to honor deities, ancestors, or natural forces, believing that wine had a power to bring them closer to the spiritual world.

Spread Through the Fertile Crescent

The area known as the Fertile Crescent stretches from the Persian Gulf up through Mesopotamia and down the Levant. It was one of the earliest centers of agriculture. It was also a place of constant trade and cultural exchange. Once people discovered wine, it quickly spread along these trade routes. Merchants found that wine was a valuable product that could be exchanged for other goods.

With the spread of wine, different regions started to develop their own styles. They used their local grapes, clay jars, and traditions. As societies in these areas grew more complex, wine started to appear at feasts, ceremonies, and even as a gift for respected visitors. This long process of sharing and trading wine prepared the foundation for the major wine cultures of Mesopotamia, Egypt, and later Greece and Rome.

How We Know: Archaeological Evidence

Much of what we know about early wine comes from items dug up by archaeologists. Pottery shards, grape seeds, and grape skin remains can be tested using a range of scientific methods. One test looks for tartaric acid, which is commonly found in grapes. Another test can find ancient residues of wine.

For example, scientists working in the South Caucasus region and in parts of the Fertile Crescent found pottery dated back thousands of years. They also found grape pips (seeds) in layers of soil that matched human settlement patterns. Additionally, some cave sites have large earthenware vessels that might have been used as fermentation chambers.

By studying these pieces of the past, researchers can make guesses about the volume of wine produced, the time of year people picked grapes, and even how they pressed or stored them. These discoveries help us imagine the daily lives of people who walked the earth many millennia ago.

Early Challenges

Making wine in ancient times was not easy. Early communities had to deal with unpredictable weather, pests, and the risk of spoilage. If the container was not sealed properly or if the grapes had too many contaminants, the wine could turn into vinegar or spoil. Also, because there was little understanding of sanitation, many batches might have been lost to mold or harmful bacteria.

Another challenge was consistency. Unlike modern times, there were no tools to measure temperature, sugar levels, or acidity. Everything was done by hand and by feel. Sometimes the wine turned out well. Other times, it might taste bad or even be unsafe. Over time, people learned better methods through trial and error, leading to improvements in wine quality.

Cultural Importance

Even with all these challenges, wine became important in many early societies. It was often seen as a sign of status, especially if only certain families or priests could afford or produce large amounts of wine. Feasts where wine was served were occasions to show off wealth and hospitality. Tribes might have used wine as a form of tribute or tax. Some leaders might have controlled the flow of wine to maintain power over their followers.

Wine also influenced art and storytelling. People carved grape vines and clusters into pottery or temple walls. They told tales of how the gods taught them to make wine or how wine gave wisdom to ancient heroes. Although these stories may have changed over time, they show that wine was not just a drink but a cultural marker.

Comparison With Other Early Fermented Drinks

Wine was not the only fermented drink in ancient times. Cultures around the world discovered that beer could be made from grains like barley or wheat. In some regions, mead was made from honey. Fermented beverages were common because they lasted longer than fresh fruit juices or milk, and the alcohol helped kill some germs that might be in water.

However, wine had a certain appeal because grapes have a unique set of flavors and aromas. Also, grapevines can grow in many hilly or rocky areas, which makes use of lands not always suitable for other crops. This adaptability helped wine become a major drink in ancient times, especially in the Mediterranean and surrounding regions.

Health Aspects

While ancient people did not have modern science, they noticed some benefits of wine. Water sources could be dirty, leading to illness. Wine, because of its acidity and alcohol, was sometimes safer to drink. Mixing a little wine into water could kill bacteria. People might have also used wine as a basic antiseptic for wounds.

Of course, wine could also lead to drunkenness if consumed in large amounts. Some early texts from later periods (like ancient Mesopotamia or Egypt) mention warnings against excessive drinking. But the sense of relaxation and mild euphoria that wine provided likely contributed to its popularity.

Connection to Later Civilizations

The earliest wine cultures laid the groundwork for more developed wine traditions in Egypt, Mesopotamia, and beyond. The idea of fermenting grape juice, storing it in containers, and sharing it at important events was passed down from these prehistoric groups. As we move forward in our journey, we will see how each civilization put its own stamp on wine culture, sometimes using wine for both daily meals and major religious events.

CHAPTER 2

Wine in Ancient Egypt

Introduction

Egypt is famous for its pyramids, pharaohs, and the Nile River. It is also known for its ancient religious beliefs and grand burial practices. Wine played a part in many of these cultural aspects. While beer was the everyday drink for many Egyptians, wine held a special place in religious ceremonies, royal feasts, and funerals. In this chapter, we will explore how wine took root in Egypt, how it was produced and used, and why it was considered an important drink.

We will see how the geography of the Nile Delta helped in grape cultivation and how Egyptian artisans and scribes left us records that show the daily life of vineyard workers. We will also learn about the relationship between wine and Egyptian religion, especially the important role it played in offerings to the gods and in the afterlife beliefs.

The Arrival of Wine in Egypt

Historians think wine came to Egypt through trade or cultural exchange. It might have come from the Levant or the eastern Mediterranean, where wine was already known. Early Egyptian rulers or traders saw its value and started to import it. Over time, Egyptian farmers learned to grow grapes along the Nile River, using the rich soil left behind by the annual floods.

As demand for wine grew, Egyptians set up vineyards in the Nile Delta region, where the soil was especially good. The mild winters and hot summers, along with irrigation canals, helped grapes thrive.

However, the climate in most parts of Egypt was too dry, so vineyards needed careful management, including watering and shading the vines as needed.

Wine Production in Ancient Egypt

Egyptian wall paintings, tomb decorations, and writings show scenes of grape cultivation, harvesting, crushing, and fermenting. These pictures provide a valuable window into Egyptian winemaking techniques.

1. **Planting and Growing Grapes**: Egyptian farmers selected areas near the Nile or in well-irrigated spots. They sometimes grew grapes on trellises to lift them off the hot ground and to make harvesting easier.

2. **Harvesting**: The Egyptians usually harvested grapes in late summer. Workers would fill baskets with bunches of ripe grapes and carry them to the press.

3. **Crushing the Grapes**: One common method was to place grapes in a large vat, where workers would stomp on them with their feet. This method gently released the juice without crushing the seeds (which could add bitterness). Sometimes, they used cloth sacks to press the grapes, twisting the sack to squeeze out the juice.

4. **Fermentation and Storage**: The juice was put into large pottery jars or amphorae. These jars were often sealed with a clay stopper or cloth to keep out bugs and dirt. Natural yeast in the environment would start fermentation. Ancient texts hint that Egyptians might have also used additives like spices or resins, although this was not as common as in other places.

5. **Labeling and Sealing**: Egyptian wine jars sometimes had seals or inscriptions that told us the vineyard name, the type of wine, or even the year of the reign of a certain pharaoh. This labeling system is one of the earliest known instances of detailed wine identification.

The Status of Wine in Egyptian Society

Wine was more costly to produce than beer, so it became a drink of the upper classes—mainly nobles, priests, and royalty. It was often featured in lavish banquets, where guests could relax while being served by attendants. These feasts sometimes lasted late into the night and included music, dancing, and plenty of food.

But wine was not entirely limited to the elite. Over time, smaller batches of local wine might have been made and drunk by middle-class families or temple workers, though likely in smaller amounts due to cost. Beer, on the other hand, was the standard daily drink for most Egyptians because it was easier to make from locally grown grains.

Religious and Funerary Uses

One of the most unique parts of Egyptian culture was its focus on the afterlife. The Egyptians believed that people lived again in another world after death. They also believed that gods played a direct role in daily life. Wine was used as an offering to the gods and as a sign of wealth and respect.

Offerings to the Gods

In many temple rituals, priests poured out wine as an offering. They believed that the gods enjoyed wine, along with incense, bread, and other gifts. Some wall reliefs show pharaohs presenting wine jars to deities. The act of giving wine symbolized a bond between humans and the divine.

Wine in the Afterlife

Egyptians placed jars of wine in tombs, especially those of pharaohs or high-status individuals. They believed that the dead would need food and drink in the afterlife. The presence of wine suggested comfort, pleasure, and a continuation of earthly delights. Some tombs even had a detailed record of the vineyard's location, the year the wine was made, and the name of the chief winemaker. This helped the deceased keep track of their earthly possessions in the spirit world.

The Symbolism of Wine

Wine in ancient Egypt carried rich symbolism. Red wine, in particular, was linked to the blood of gods or certain myths. In some stories, the goddess Hathor (associated with love, joy, and motherhood) was also linked to drunkenness and festivity. Wine was thus not just a physical drink but also had spiritual layers of meaning.

Some myths talk about the lioness goddess Sekhmet, who was calmed down when the sun god Ra tricked her into drinking beer or wine mixed with red dye, causing her to become drunk and abandon her rage. This story shows how the Egyptians understood the power of alcohol to change behavior, both for good and for potential chaos.

Egyptian Wine Varieties

While Egyptians did not have the same modern idea of "varietals," they did recognize differences in wine based on region and year. The Nile Delta had several known vineyard sites, each possibly with a unique flavor profile due to soil, climate, and grape type. Some historical references talk about wines from places like the Mareotic region (near Alexandria) being especially fine.

Other Egyptian records mention sweet wines or lighter, more acidic wines. Some may have been white, while others were more red or even closer to what we might call rosé. Because the Egyptian climate is hot, making wine required special care to prevent spoilage, so certain regions became famous for producing higher quality wines.

Wine at the Royal Court

Pharaohs and their families drank wine at royal banquets, with music, dance, and poetry as entertainment. These events showed the pharaoh's wealth and power. High-ranking officials and foreign guests would attend, and large jars of wine were poured into smaller cups. Servants would move among the guests, refilling cups and making sure everyone had enough to eat and drink.

Sometimes, these gatherings were also a place for diplomacy. When foreign dignitaries visited, Egyptian rulers would serve them the best wines, hoping to impress them. Likewise, Egyptian envoys might bring wine as a gift to neighboring kingdoms, showing Egypt's bounty and skill in winemaking.

Daily Life of Vineyard Workers

While the upper classes enjoyed wine, the people who produced it often lived simpler lives. Egyptian tomb paintings also show scenes of farm laborers tending vines, carrying baskets of grapes, or pressing them. These pictures are some of the oldest detailed depictions of vineyard work in the ancient world.

Workers had to deal with the hot sun, possible insect infestations, and the need to carefully water the vines. During harvest season, many laborers would gather at the vineyards to pick the grapes quickly before they spoiled. After the harvest, they would help with pressing and storing the wine. The success of the harvest could mean a greater supply of wine, which was good for both the workers and the vineyard owners.

Beer vs. Wine: A Quick Look

In Egypt, beer was the common drink for everyday life. Barley was plentiful, and the process to make beer was straightforward. Beer also spoiled less quickly than fruit-based drinks in that hot climate. Wine, meanwhile, was more expensive to produce and usually reserved for special events.

Yet, wine had a special place in religion, royalty, and the afterlife. Beer could be used for offerings too, but wine was seen as more prestigious. Even so, some texts refer to wine as a possible source of trouble if a person drank too much. The Egyptians understood that wine could lead to both celebration and problems.

Trade and Influence

Egypt's location along major trade routes allowed its wine culture to influence neighboring lands. Egyptian wine was shipped to the Levant and other parts of the Mediterranean. In return, Egypt imported wines from places like Canaan. This exchange helped spread different grape varieties and winemaking knowledge.

Egyptian culture also influenced how wine was stored and labeled in other regions. Many amphorae and jars found in ancient shipwrecks or trade ports show Egyptian-inspired designs or inscriptions. Through trade, the Egyptians introduced their customs and tastes to the broader ancient world.

Archaeological Discoveries

Modern archaeologists have found wine presses and vats in places such as the Nile Delta. They have also discovered tombs with sealed jars of wine that retained residue. Analysis of this residue gives clues about the types of grapes, possible additives, and the age of the wine. The presence of detailed hieroglyphs on some jars shows just how carefully Egyptians documented their wine. This kind of record-keeping helps us better understand how sophisticated their wine production really was.

Legacy of Egyptian Wine

Although Egyptians are more widely known for their pyramids and mummies, their wine tradition was advanced for its time. They developed irrigation systems that allowed vineyards to exist in a harsh climate. They created stable containers for fermentation and storage, and they labeled wine jars with vineyard and date information. Their beliefs and customs gave wine a unique place in society, linking it to gods, the afterlife, and royal power.

By the time Egypt moved into later dynasties and eventually came under Greek and Roman influence, wine was already a well-established part of Egyptian culture. Future conquerors, such as Alexander the Great and then the Romans, found a region that understood viticulture (the growing of grapes) and had a strong love of wine. This heritage would blend with Greek and Roman practices, further shaping the story of wine around the Mediterranean.

CHAPTER 3

The World of Mesopotamia and Wine's Growth

3.1 Introduction

Mesopotamia is often called the "Cradle of Civilization." This region covers parts of what is now Iraq, Kuwait, eastern Syria, and southeastern Turkey. The name "Mesopotamia" comes from Greek words meaning "land between rivers," referring to the Tigris and Euphrates Rivers. These rivers brought water to a largely dry place, allowing people to farm, build cities, and create some of the oldest known civilizations.

When we think of Mesopotamia, we often think of the Sumerians, Babylonians, and Assyrians. These groups gave us cuneiform writing, law codes, and grand structures like ziggurats. But what about wine? Many might believe beer was the main drink there—indeed, beer was very popular. However, wine also had a significant presence in Mesopotamia, especially among the wealthy and the ruling classes.

In this chapter, we will look at how wine found its way into daily life, religion, and trade in Mesopotamia. We will also see how the land's climate posed some challenges for growing grapes, and how people overcame these barriers. By exploring old tablets, archaeological evidence, and the writings of different city-states, we will learn how wine continued to grow in importance over time.

3.2 The Land of Mesopotamia: Climate and Geography

Mesopotamia had a hot, dry climate for much of the year. It also lacked many natural resources like timber or precious metals.

However, the Tigris and Euphrates Rivers flooded seasonally, bringing rich silt to the plains. This silt helped farmers grow grains, fruits, and vegetables.

Still, grapevines are not as easy to cultivate in flat, hot lands as they are in cooler, hilly regions. In many parts of Mesopotamia, grapes had to be brought from areas with more favorable conditions, such as the foothills to the north or the mountainous regions to the northeast. Over time, people built irrigation canals to help grow different crops, including grapevines, even in places that did not naturally support them.

Because of these difficulties, wine was often more expensive than beer. Beer could be produced from grain—barley especially—which grew well in this region. Wine, however, required extra labor and sometimes had to be imported from neighboring lands where grapes thrived. Despite these hurdles, wine began to hold a special place at royal courts and religious gatherings.

Trading Networks

Mesopotamia developed extensive trading networks, reaching out to regions like the Levant (the Eastern Mediterranean), Anatolia (modern-day Turkey), and the Zagros Mountains (part of present-day Iran). From these areas, merchants brought in timber, metals, and often wine. Trade routes by land and along rivers made it possible to transport goods in bulk, though it was not always easy.

Wines from certain regions became well-known for their flavor or color, much like how certain wines today are famous for their origin. Even in ancient times, people recognized that grapes from cooler, hillier regions produced better wine. Mesopotamian tablets sometimes mention shipments of wine as part of taxes or tributes given to local rulers.

3.3 Sumerian Beginnings

Early City-States

The Sumerians were among the first major groups in southern Mesopotamia, founding city-states like Uruk, Ur, and Eridu (around 4000–3000 BCE). They built impressive temples and ziggurats and developed one of the earliest known writing systems: cuneiform. Most references to drinks in Sumerian texts focus on beer, which was common in daily life. However, there are scattered hints that wine was also present, though less accessible.

Wine in Sumerian Records

Some Sumerian tablets mention fruit pressed for juices, including grape juice. Tablets used a system of wedge-shaped symbols, so translations can be tricky. Still, a few signs may refer specifically to wine. For example, there might be a symbol for "vineyard" or "wine" in certain administrative lists. These records often list how much wine was given to temple priests or used in offerings to gods.

Because wine was rarer, it often shows up in records about temples or the palace. Temple complexes in Sumerian cities served as economic hubs, where people offered goods to the gods. Wine might have been seen as a luxury drink suitable for divine beings or for feasts celebrating special holidays.

Religious and Ceremonial Roles

The Sumerians believed in a pantheon of gods who controlled natural forces. Large temple estates ran a variety of agricultural projects, possibly including vineyards. When Sumerian priests performed rituals, they might pour out small amounts of wine as a libation—an offering poured on the ground or over an altar—to honor the gods.

Feasts in Sumerian temples might include bread, fruit, meat, and drinks like beer and wine. Archaeological evidence—like cups, drinking vessels, and references to various beverages—suggests that ceremonies often involved participants sharing these drinks. Wine might have been saved for high-ranking officials, priests, or special guests because it was more costly.

Social and Economic Impact

For ordinary Sumerian people, wine was not a daily drink. Because it was expensive, they might encounter wine only at significant events, such as religious festivals or maybe a wedding. Wealthy families, however, could afford to stock wine at home or receive wine as gifts from traders.

Over time, as the Sumerians expanded their trade, they became more familiar with wine-producing regions. They may have started cultivating grapes wherever the climate permitted. These early efforts laid the foundation for later Mesopotamian cultures that would embrace wine in more direct ways.

3.4 Babylonian Times

Rise of Babylon

After the Sumerian city-states, Babylon rose to prominence in central Mesopotamia. Babylon became famous under King Hammurabi (around the 18th century BCE) and later under King Nebuchadnezzar II (6th century BCE). The city boasted grand walls, temples, and the fabled Hanging Gardens (though their exact historical reality is debated).

During Babylon's height, trade and culture thrived. Merchants passing through Babylon brought goods from distant lands. This included grapes and wine, which were stored in large jars or containers. Babylon's rulers also sent out diplomatic gifts, sometimes including local specialties or items they had obtained through trade.

Expanding Vineyards

By the time of Babylon's growth, people had learned more about building irrigation canals. In certain parts of Mesopotamia, they tried to establish vineyards, though it was still not as widespread as grain farming. Some records show that wealthy landowners or temples managed plots of grapevines. Workers had to maintain these vines carefully, protecting them from scorching heat.

The Babylonians also recorded deliveries of wine for palace use. Some inscriptions detail how many jars of wine arrived, who delivered them, and what they might be used for. These administrative notes reveal that Babylon had a structured system to distribute food and drinks, including wine, to royal officials and temple staff.

Wine in the Palace

Babylon's kings and nobles enjoyed banquets in their grand halls. Guests would be served an array of dishes: roasted meats, vegetables, fruits, and baked goods. Wine was on the menu for those who could afford it. Servants would pour wine from large jars into cups, ensuring that the important people had enough to drink.

Because wine was often imported or grown with difficulty, it became a sign of wealth and power. Sharing wine with foreign diplomats showed Babylon's prosperity and refinement. Rulers might have used these gatherings as opportunities to negotiate treaties or show off their luxurious lifestyle to visiting dignitaries.

Religious Use in Babylon

Like the Sumerians before them, the Babylonians had many gods. Chief among them was Marduk, who was honored in large temple festivals. Priests performed rituals that included offerings of food and drink. Wine was a special gift, symbolizing respect and gratitude to the gods.

Priests kept careful records of offerings, including how much wine was provided. Sometimes, wine was poured over altars or used to wash statues of the gods. Even though beer remained common among the lower classes, the use of wine in religious ceremonies helped preserve its special status.

3.5 Wine and Religion in Mesopotamia

Many Gods, Many Celebrations

Mesopotamia's religious life was deeply woven into everyday activities. People believed that each city had a patron god or goddess watching over it. Temples often served as the economic and spiritual centers of these cities. During major festivals, local inhabitants gathered for processions, sacrifices, and feasts.

While beer was given to the masses, wine often appeared at the high point of these events, possibly shared by priests and ruling officials. This pattern reflected wine's rarity. It also gave these gatherings an air of importance—wine drinking marked a moment of honor for the gods.

Mythologies Involving Wine

While direct stories about wine are less abundant than in, say, Greek myths, some Mesopotamian tales mention drinks that could be similar to wine. In the *Epic of Gilgamesh*, we meet a tavern keeper named Siduri, who offers Gilgamesh advice. Though the drink in question is typically thought to be beer, references to a special type of beverage can sometimes be interpreted as wine. Because these stories are very old and the translations can be uncertain, it is not always clear which type of alcohol they refer to.

What is clear is that Mesopotamians recognized the pleasant effects of strong drink. They also knew these effects could lead to excess. Like many other ancient cultures, they had words of caution about drinking too much, which could result in foolish behavior or shame.

Temple Wine Storage

Archaeological excavations at some Mesopotamian sites show evidence of storage areas, possibly for large pots or jars that contained wine. Temples often managed their own land, including vineyards if the environment allowed. They might also receive wine as a tax or tribute. This wine was kept for rituals or for special visitors, including local leaders.

Temple records might describe the daily distribution of bread, oil, beer, and wine to priests, workers, and officials. In these lists, wine often appears as a smaller portion compared to other staples, again showing its premium status.

3.6 The Code of Hammurabi and Its Insights

Hammurabi's Laws

Hammurabi was a famous Babylonian king who created a detailed law code around 1750 BCE. The Code of Hammurabi is one of the earliest known sets of written laws. It covers topics like trade, property rights, marriage, and even the wages of workers.

Though beer is mentioned more often in Mesopotamian texts, some parts of Hammurabi's Code involve taverns or the sale of beverages. These laws regulated how owners of drinking establishments should conduct business and how they should handle money and customers. While most references point to beer, the broader category of "strong drink" could include wine as well.

Regulating Taverns

In one well-known law, tavern owners—often women—were held responsible for the behavior of customers. If criminals met in a tavern and the owner did not report this, she could be punished. Though beer was the primary drink sold in these places, wine might also have been available at a higher price.

The Code of Hammurabi also set prices and exchange rates for goods, which might include wine in certain references. By regulating these businesses, the Babylonian state tried to maintain fairness and order in commerce. This shows us that wine and other alcoholic drinks were not just items of enjoyment—they also played an economic and social role.

Social Class and Drink

Hammurabi's laws help us see that Mesopotamian society was divided by class. Slaves, free commoners, and nobility all had different levels of wealth and access to luxuries. Wine fits into this picture as a drink mostly enjoyed by the wealthy and by religious leaders. The code aimed to prevent dishonest dealings in alcohol, meaning that even in ancient times, the authorities knew that such businesses had to be carefully watched to prevent scams or public disorder.

3.7 Social Life and Wine

Banquets and Feasts

The people of Mesopotamia, especially those in higher classes, loved grand feasts. These gatherings took place for religious festivals, weddings, coronations, or victory celebrations after a successful military campaign. Guests wore fine clothes, and servants brought out trays of food like roasted sheep or goat, bread, fruits, and sweets made from dates or honey.

Wine was served in cups or small bowls. Because of the limited supply, servers might ration it. The host, often a wealthy noble or a member of the royal family, made sure to show generosity by offering wine to special guests. This act raised the host's social status, as it displayed an ability to secure and share a luxury product.

Gift Exchanges

In Mesopotamia, giving gifts was part of diplomacy. Rulers exchanged valuable items to keep alliances strong or to appease more powerful kings. Wine could be one of those gifts. A ruler might send fine wine from a favored region, along with expensive textiles or metals. In return, they might get horses, timber, or precious stones.

These gift exchanges served as a way to show friendship or loyalty. If a king received fine wine, it suggested the other side respected him enough to send a costly good. The event of receiving these gifts was sometimes recorded on clay tablets, marking the quantity and origin of the wine.

Everyday Drinking?

Most ordinary Mesopotamians drank beer daily because it was cheap and easy to produce. Wine, however, did appear in some households, especially among the middle classes who could afford small amounts. Doctors sometimes recommended wine for certain ailments, though references to medical uses are sparse.

Wine also appears in some personal letters. For instance, a merchant might write to a family member asking them to send a jar of wine for a special occasion. These letters, preserved on clay tablets, show that wine was not just for the elite, but it was still special enough to be treated as a valuable item.

3.8 Archaeological Clues

Pottery and Storage Jars

Archaeologists have discovered large pottery jars in several Mesopotamian digs. Some of these jars had residues that, when tested, indicated the presence of tartaric acid and other substances linked to fermented grape juice. These findings suggest that wine was stored in large containers, not too different from the amphorae used by later civilizations.

Seals and inscriptions on these jars sometimes mention the contents. For instance, a jar might be marked with a symbol for "wine," or it might detail who owned it. These clues give us direct proof that wine was part of trade and storage practices in Mesopotamia.

Vineyard Remains

In a few places, archaeologists have found evidence that might point to old vineyards or wine presses. While these remains are less common than those found in lands known primarily for wine (like the Levant or the Caucasus), they confirm that some grape cultivation occurred in Mesopotamia itself. Irrigation channels, vineyard posts, or tools for crushing grapes can be pieced together to form a picture of local wine production.

Written Records

Cuneiform tablets discovered in palace archives or temple storerooms provide another layer of evidence. Some of these tablets list rations of wine given to temple workers, gifts for visiting officials, or the trade of wine in exchange for other goods. By studying these texts, historians learn about the economic role of wine, the value placed on it, and how it moved around the region.

3.9 The Assyrian Influence

Assyrian Empire

North of Babylon was Assyria, a powerful empire known for its fierce armies and massive construction projects. The Assyrians rose to power around the 14th century BCE and had periods of strong control over much of Mesopotamia until around the 7th century BCE. Cities like Nineveh and Nimrud became centers of politics and culture.

Royal Palaces and Gardens

Assyrian kings built huge palaces decorated with carved stone reliefs that showed scenes of hunting, warfare, and royal life. Some of these reliefs depict banquets and possibly the serving of wine. Assyria also had royal gardens, which sometimes included vines or fruit trees. While the climate was challenging, the Assyrians learned to bring water from rivers to these gardens, creating lush displays of plants.

Military Campaigns and Wine

The Assyrians were known for expanding their territory through conquests. By controlling many regions, including those with better conditions for grape growing, they could secure a steady supply of wine. Returning armies sometimes brought back spoils, which might include wine or vineyard workers captured in battle.

In some letters from the Assyrian period, officials talk about shipments of wine to the royal court. These shipments had to be of good quality to please the king. Failure to deliver on time or to meet standards could result in punishment. This level of strictness shows how important wine was at the royal table.

Cultural Exchange

When the Assyrians conquered lands that produced wine, they brought new methods back to their heartland. They also introduced their own customs to the conquered people. Through this exchange, wine-making knowledge spread further. Over time, various groups in the region picked up new techniques for planting vines, pressing grapes, and storing wine.

3.10 Legacy and Conclusion

Influence on Neighboring Regions

Mesopotamia was a crossroads of trade and culture. Even though it did not have the best climate for large-scale viticulture, it played a key role in spreading wine across the Middle East. Through trade networks, treaties, and conquests, wine made its way into many aspects of life, from royal banquets to religious ceremonies. Neighboring lands, such as the Levant and Anatolia, also learned from Mesopotamian practices. In turn, Mesopotamians borrowed techniques and grapes from those lands.

Beyond Beer

It is true that Mesopotamia is more famous for its beer culture. Yet, as we have seen, wine was also part of this grand civilization. It might not have been as common, but it had significant symbolic and social weight. People used it to honor gods, impress rulers, and mark special occasions. The presence of wine in one of the world's oldest civilizations shows how humans everywhere craved new tastes and experiences.

Stepping Stone to Other Civilizations

As Babylon and Assyria eventually fell to new powers (like the Persians), wine continued its journey, influencing the habits of each new empire that rose in this region. The knowledge of making and storing wine spread throughout the Near East. By the time the Greeks and later the Romans came into contact with these lands, they found well-established wine cultures that contributed to their own traditions.

CHAPTER 4

Wine in Ancient Greece

4.1 Introduction

Ancient Greece is often celebrated for its art, philosophy, democracy (in some city-states), and mythology. It also had a deep love for wine. In fact, the Greeks revered a wine god, Dionysus (also known as Bacchus by the Romans later on). Greek poets wrote about wine, and Greeks developed social gatherings called "symposia" that revolved around drinking wine and sharing ideas.

In this chapter, we will explore how wine became central to Greek culture. We will see how geographic features, such as mountains and islands, influenced grape growing. We will also learn about the Greek habit of mixing wine with water and the special pottery they used. Most importantly, we will see how wine was connected to Greek religion, daily life, and trade.

4.2 Geography and Grapes in Greece

The Land of Mountains and Sea

Greece is made up of a mainland peninsula and many islands. Much of the land is hilly or mountainous. The climate is Mediterranean, meaning summers are dry and hot, while winters are mild with some rainfall. This climate, combined with rocky soil, turned out to be excellent for certain types of grapevines.

Unlike the flat plains of Mesopotamia, Greek valleys and hillsides provided good drainage. Grapevines do not like to have "wet feet," meaning their roots do best when excess water can flow away. The

Greek islands also benefited from coastal breezes that cooled the vines during hot summers. All these factors allowed Greek farmers to grow many varieties of grapes suited for wine.

Early Vineyards

The earliest Greek-speaking peoples likely learned about wine from their contacts with older civilizations like the Minoans on Crete (around 2000–1400 BCE). The Minoans, in turn, had trade links with Egypt and the Levant. As Greek culture evolved on the mainland, grape growing spread from the Aegean islands to regions like Attica, the Peloponnese, and Thessaly.

Homer, the legendary poet (believed to have lived around the 8th century BCE), mentions wine in his epic poems *The Iliad* and *The Odyssey*. These works show that by Homer's time, wine was already common in Greek life. Later city-states, such as Athens and Sparta, also farmed vineyards and gained wealth by exporting wine to other areas.

4.3 The Role of Dionysus

God of Wine and Festivity

In Greek mythology, Dionysus was the god of wine, fertility, and religious ecstasy. Stories say that he traveled widely, teaching people how to grow vines and make wine. He was often shown as a young man wearing a wreath of ivy or grape leaves, carrying a staff topped with pine cones, called a "thyrsus."

Festivals in Dionysus's honor were major events in many Greek city-states. These festivals included plays (tragedies and comedies), processions, music, and, of course, plenty of wine. Greeks believed that Dionysus could bring joy and unity through wine, but also madness if taken too far.

Religious Ceremonies

Wine featured in many Greek rituals, not just those for Dionysus. The Greeks poured wine as libations to honor all kinds of gods and heroes. In some public ceremonies, officials would pour out wine, asking the gods for blessings or victory in war. Sometimes, they would mix wine with water and a bit of barley to make a special drink used in sacred rites.

At home, families also made small offerings of wine at household altars. They might pour a few drops before drinking to thank the gods. This small gesture shows how woven wine was into daily religious practice.

4.4 The Symposium: A Social Institution

What Is a Symposium?

A symposium was a structured drinking party that took place in men's quarters of a Greek house. Guests, usually male citizens, would recline on couches arranged around the room. Slaves or servants filled cups with wine, which was almost always mixed with water. The Greeks thought drinking unmixed wine was barbaric or dangerous, leading to quick drunkenness.

During the symposium, participants would share in conversation, recite poetry, sing songs, and even play games like "kottabos," which involved flicking drops of wine at targets. Sometimes, philosophers discussed serious topics about life, the universe, or ethics. Other times, the focus was purely on fun and companionship.

Wine Mixing and Etiquette

Greeks rarely drank wine straight from the jar. They thought that pure wine was too strong. Instead, they used a large bowl called a "krater" to mix wine with water. The host decided the ratio—often one part wine to two or three parts water. This ritual mixing had practical reasons, as it helped control how quickly people got drunk.

The symposium also had a leader or "symposiarch," who guided the flow of wine, decided when to refill cups, and sometimes set rules for toasting or conversation. This person was responsible for keeping order and ensuring guests did not drink too much too fast. The aim was balanced enjoyment, not wild excess.

Cultural Importance

Symposia were more than just parties. They were vital in shaping Greek culture, politics, and philosophy. Many thinkers like Plato, Aristotle, or Socrates used symposia to share ideas in a relaxed setting. Plays, poems, and philosophical works mention symposia as places where minds could meet and express creativity.

Women, except for entertainers or courtesans, were typically excluded from symposia in most city-states. This custom shows the social norms of ancient Greece, where men held the main political and cultural roles. Even so, the symposium remained central to how Greeks bonded and communicated.

4.5 Types of Greek Wine and Pottery

Regional Varieties

Ancient Greece had many wine regions, each with its own character. Some islands like Chios and Thasos became famous for producing strong, sweet wines. The rocky slopes of the mainland also gave certain wines distinct flavors. Greeks observed that soil, weather, and grape variety mattered in the final taste, though they did not use the modern term "terroir."

They also learned methods to preserve wine, like adding resin from pine trees. This produced a flavored wine that we might call "retsina" today, though modern retsina is different in style. The resin acted as a sealant, helping stop the wine from spoiling quickly. It also gave the wine a distinctive pine-like taste.

Pottery and Storage

Greeks were master potters, making many types of vessels for wine:

- **Amphorae**: tall jars with two handles, used for storage and transport. They often had narrow necks to reduce contact with air.
- **Krater**: a large bowl for mixing wine and water.
- **Kylix**: a shallow drinking cup with a wide rim, often used in symposia.
- **Kantharos**: a cup with high handles associated with Dionysus.

Greek artisans decorated these vessels with scenes from mythology, daily life, and of course, wine-drinking parties. Amphorae could also have painted labels or stamps indicating the origin of the wine.

Seals and Trade Marks

Many Greek amphorae discovered in shipwrecks or archaeological sites carry stamps or inscriptions. These might show the city or island where the wine came from, or the name of the potter or merchant. This allowed trade partners to recognize high-quality wines. Some city-states, like Rhodes, became known for their amphora stamps, showing how far Greek wine traveled across the Mediterranean.

4.6 Wine and Greek Trade

Expanding Across the Seas

The Greeks were skilled sailors and traders. By 800 BCE, they had begun establishing colonies around the Mediterranean and Black Sea to secure resources, farmland, and trade opportunities. These colonies also spread Greek culture, including wine-making knowledge. Vineyards popped up in coastal areas of southern Italy, Sicily, and parts of what is now France and Spain, as well as in Asia Minor (modern-day Turkey).

Greek merchants carried wine in amphorae on ships. Along with olive oil and pottery, wine was one of the main exports. In exchange, Greeks might receive grain, timber, metals, and slaves from other regions. This trade boosted the economy of many city-states and introduced Greek wine to different cultures.

Wine as a Diplomatic Tool

Just like in Mesopotamia or Egypt, wine served as a valuable diplomatic gift in Greece. When city-states made alliances or sought to avoid conflict, they might exchange goods, including fine wines. Serving imported Greek wine at a banquet could impress guests from another city or kingdom.

Spreading Wine Culture

As Greek colonies flourished, locals learned about Greek ways of vine cultivation. Over generations, these areas developed their own wine styles, sometimes mixing local grape varieties with Greek ones. The Greek appetite for wine and willingness to trade it contributed to the drink's spread far and wide. This pattern continued even when the Roman civilization later took over much of the Mediterranean world.

4.7 Daily Life and Wine

Household Consumption

Not everyone in ancient Greece had lavish banquets. Many small farmers and artisans drank wine at home with simple meals of bread, olives, cheese, or fish. However, because wine was often mixed with water, the strength would vary. For some families, wine was a regular part of dinner, seen as more hygienic than plain water, which could be polluted.

Greek women, particularly in Athens, lived more secluded lives than men. While they might not attend symposia, they still had access to wine at home for personal use, religious ceremonies, or family meals. Over time, social norms changed from city-state to city-state, so practices varied.

Festivals and Public Events

In addition to private symposia, there were many public gatherings where wine flowed freely. The festival called "Anthesteria" in Athens celebrated Dionysus with three days of parties, including drinking contests and the opening of new wine jars from the harvest. People wore flower garlands and visited each other's homes to share wine.

At theatrical performances, which were also part of religious festivals, audiences might have some wine as they watched new tragedies or comedies. This made the event more festive. The bond between wine, drama, and the worship of Dionysus was very strong in Greek society.

4.8 Philosophers and Wine

Wine as a Topic of Thought

Greek philosophers sometimes wrote about wine's effects and place in society. For example, Plato in some dialogues talks about how wine can reveal a person's true character. He also discusses the right amount of wine for a gathering—enough to relax people without causing chaos.

Aristotle, on the other hand, looked at wine in terms of moderation and self-control. He recognized that drunkenness could lead to moral and social problems. However, he also saw value in the camaraderie wine could create if consumed responsibly. These discussions show that wine had become deeply connected to social and ethical thinking among the Greek intellectuals.

Symposia as Intellectual Spaces

Famous conversations, like those described in Plato's *Symposium*, show how wine could spark lively debate. In this particular dialogue, Socrates and other thinkers discuss the nature of love, all while reclining at a drinking party. By mixing wine and conversation, the participants found a relaxed environment to share ideas about the divine, beauty, and virtue.

This blend of social pleasure and intellectual discussion became a hallmark of Greek culture. Later societies would imitate the Greek symposium in their own versions of salons or literary gatherings. Wine played the role of social lubricant, making these deep talks feel less formal and more open.

4.9 Mythology, Art, and Wine

Dionysian Imagery

Greek artists created countless images of Dionysus, satyrs (his half-goat companions), and maenads (his wild female followers) in sculpture and vase paintings. These images often showed lively scenes of revelry, dancing, and the pouring of wine. Some pottery pieces found in tombs or temples display entire stories related to Dionysus and his entourage.

The Theater and Wine

The theater festivals held in honor of Dionysus included performances of tragedies by playwrights like Aeschylus, Sophocles, and Euripides, as well as comedies by Aristophanes. While the plays themselves were not just about wine, they were performed during celebrations of the wine god. The audience, having enjoyed a bit of wine, laughed and cried along with the dramas, creating a communal experience that was part religious, part cultural entertainment.

The Vine as a Symbol

The grapevine and its clusters appeared on coins, reliefs, and other art objects. It became a symbol not just of Dionysus but also of the abundance and cultural achievements of Greece. When a city-state minted coins with vine imagery, it sometimes wanted to boast about its wine production or connect itself to the broader Greek identity that prized wine.

4.10 Legacy and Transition

Influence on Rome

The ancient Greeks passed on their love and knowledge of wine to the Romans. When Rome began to expand, it came into contact with Greek colonies in southern Italy and Sicily. The Romans learned much from these Greek outposts about grape growing, storing wine, and hosting elaborate banquets. Roman wine culture, which we will explore in a later chapter, owes a lot to the Greeks.

Spread of Greek Wine Culture

Greek traders and settlers took their winemaking practices to other parts of Europe and Asia Minor. Over centuries, this helped shape regional wine styles and traditions. Even after Greek city-states lost independence to the Macedonians and then to Rome, local people kept their vineyards and methods. Greeks continued to make wine, pass on their traditions, and celebrate Dionysus well into the Hellenistic age (after Alexander the Great's conquests) and beyond.

Lasting Impact on Western Thought

The idea of the symposium, as a place for both drinking wine and serious discussion, had a long-lasting impact on Western culture. Future intellectual gatherings, whether in the Roman Empire or during the Renaissance, mirrored this blend of conviviality and debate. Greek plays and myths about Dionysus also influenced art and literature for thousands of years.

CHAPTER 5

The Roman Empire and Wine

5.1 Introduction

The Roman Empire was one of the largest and most influential empires in the ancient world. It stretched from Britain to parts of the Middle East and North Africa. Romans built roads, conquered lands, and united many cultures under their rule. One of the key ways they spread their culture was through their love of wine.

Romans learned much from the Greeks about growing grapevines and making wine, but they also developed their own methods. They improved large-scale wine production and made wine part of their daily life. People in every social class—from wealthy senators to ordinary farmers—came to see wine as a basic staple, though the quality and availability varied widely.

In this chapter, we will look at how Romans farmed grapes, produced wine in large quantities, and used wine in both religious ceremonies and everyday meals. We will see how Roman trade routes helped wine travel all across the empire, and how Roman laws and customs shaped the wine industry. By the end, you will understand why the Roman Empire was so important to the history of wine.

5.2 Roman Expansion and the Spread of Vineyards

5.2.1 Conquest and Infrastructure

The Romans were known for building straight roads, establishing stable governments, and creating new cities wherever they went. As the Roman armies conquered regions like Gaul (modern-day France), Hispania (Spain), and parts of central Europe, they brought their lifestyle with them. That often included setting up vineyards.

Romans believed in the benefits of wine—both for health (in small amounts) and for pleasure. Soldiers stationed in new provinces often wanted wine like they had back home. Traders saw this need as a chance to make money. They either imported wine from Italy or planted vines in the newly conquered lands. Over time, provinces like Gaul became famous for their local wines, which started as Roman-driven projects but grew into local traditions.

5.2.2 Climate and Local Adaptation

The Roman Empire covered many kinds of climates: hot and dry in North Africa, cool and damp in northern Britain, and mild in Gaul and Italy. Grapevines do best in places that have distinct seasons—warm summers and mild to cool winters. Some regions, like modern-day southern France or parts of Spain, were ideal for vines. In cooler areas like Britain, wine production was more challenging, though Romans did attempt to cultivate vines there on a limited scale.

Because of these different climates, local farmers had to adjust how they cared for vines. They learned which grape types worked best in their soil and weather. Romans also introduced irrigation in some areas, brought new vine cuttings from Italy, and taught local people pruning and harvest techniques. Over generations, these vineyards adapted to each region, creating a wide range of wine styles throughout the empire.

5.2.3 Veteran Colonies

Rome had a system where soldiers who served in the army for many years could retire and receive plots of land, often in conquered territories. These settlements, called "veteran colonies," sometimes included vineyards. Since many Roman soldiers enjoyed wine, they put effort into establishing grapevines near their new homes. This further spread Roman wine culture into every corner of the empire.

5.3 Grape Varieties and Vine Cultivation in Rome

5.3.1 Famous Roman Grape Types

Romans recognized different grape varieties, though they did not classify them like modern winemakers do. Still, ancient texts mention names of grapes that were admired for their flavor, color, or suitability for making certain types of wine. Some grapes produced sweet wines, while others produced drier styles. Many of these varieties have disappeared or evolved into new ones over the centuries, but we do know the Romans highly valued diversity in grapes.

A few famous names from Roman writings include:

- **Aminea**: A grape believed to produce high-quality, long-lasting wines.
- **Nomentana**: Grown near Rome, sometimes used for everyday drinking.
- **Apiana**: Said to attract bees due to its sweet juice, possibly used for sweeter wines.

These grapes might not be exactly the same as modern vines, but they reflect how Romans appreciated the fact that different vines had different qualities. They wrote about how some grapes ripened early, while others did well in cooler conditions.

5.3.2 Farming Methods

Romans were skilled agriculturalists. They wrote detailed guides on how to farm grapes efficiently. Important Roman authors like Cato,

Varro, and Columella created manuals advising vineyard owners on topics like choosing the right slope, spacing vines, and pruning. They recommended that vines be given enough room so that they could soak up sunlight but still allow good airflow to prevent rot.

Romans often trained vines on wooden stakes or small trellises, unlike the Greeks who sometimes used trees for support. Roman farmers discovered that controlling how vines grew, and removing unwanted shoots, produced healthier vines and better-tasting grapes. Proper pruning was key to preventing the vine from becoming too leafy and wasting its energy on unneeded growth.

5.3.3 Harvest and Labor

During the Roman harvest, large teams of workers or slaves would pick grapes by hand. On big estates, labor was carefully organized to get the grapes picked at the ideal moment. Grapes that were under-ripe or spoiled were discarded. The rest were taken quickly to wine presses, often located right in the vineyard or nearby.

Because slavery was common in ancient Rome, many vineyards relied on enslaved people to do much of the hard work. Wealthy landowners viewed vineyards as a source of profit, so they invested in good equipment and housing for the workers, though living conditions varied widely. Smaller farms often relied on family labor, with parents and children helping out during the busy harvest season.

5.4 Roman Wine Production Methods

5.4.1 Pressing Grapes

Romans used different methods for crushing grapes. One common approach was a large stone or wooden press that squeezed the grapes to release juice. Sometimes, workers first stomped on grapes with their feet in a shallow container, then placed the pulp under a press to extract even more juice.

They collected the free-run juice—that is, the first juice that flows without pressing—separately because it was considered the finest quality. The pressed juice, known as "second pressing," was often used for cheaper wines. Romans recognized that the juice from crushed seeds or stems could add harsh flavors, so they tried to manage how roughly they pressed the fruit.

5.4.2 Fermentation and Storage

After pressing, the juice went into large vats or clay jars (similar to the Greek amphora) for fermentation. Romans were aware that fermentation produced foam and gases, so they left some space in each container to prevent overflow. They typically sealed these containers with lids or clay stoppers. Natural yeast, present on grape skins or in the environment, started the fermentation process.

Temperature control was basic. Romans might keep the jars in cool cellars or partially bury them in the ground to shield them from the hot sun. Fermentation could last a few days to a couple of weeks, depending on the sugar level of the grapes and the temperature.

5.4.3 Flavoring and Sweetening

Romans often flavored their wines with herbs, spices, or resins. They might add honey for sweetness, creating a drink sometimes called "mulsum." They also produced strong sweet wines by allowing grapes to dry in the sun before pressing them, increasing their sugar content. Some texts mention adding seawater or salt to wine to change the taste and help preserve it.

Romans also made a beverage called "posca" by mixing sour wine or vinegar with water and herbs. It was common among soldiers and lower-class citizens because it was cheap and safer than drinking plain water in areas where water might be contaminated.

5.4.4 Aging and Amphorae

High-quality Roman wines were sometimes aged for years in sealed amphorae or large clay containers. Wealthy Romans might keep special vintages in their cellars, bragging about how old or rare their wines were. Poorer households, on the other hand, drank new wine soon after fermentation.

Romans labeled some amphorae with information such as the vineyard location, the year, or the consul who was in power at the time. This was an early form of vintage dating, which helped people know how old the wine was and where it came from. Over time, well-aged wines like **Falernian** became legendary, mentioned by writers such as Horace and Pliny the Elder.

5.5 Social Aspects: Banquets, Feasts, and Everyday Life

5.5.1 Roman Banquets

Wealthy Romans enjoyed large feasts called "convivia." Like the Greek symposium, these were social events with fine food, music, and conversation. However, Roman banquets could be even more elaborate, with several courses of exotic dishes. Servants brought out trays of meats, vegetables, and pastries, and poured wine into cups for guests.

Unlike the Greeks, Romans did not always mix their wine with water, though the practice did exist. Some Romans drank strong wine to show off their status—because they could afford the best wines—and also to demonstrate their ability to handle alcohol. However, these habits varied by personal preference and by custom in different parts of the empire.

5.5.2 Types of Wine Served

At a banquet, the host might start with a lighter or simpler wine, and then bring out a famous vintage to impress guests. Sweet wines could appear at the end of the meal, served with desserts or fruit. Wealthy hosts would also supply spiced or honeyed wines to add variety.

Since social hierarchy mattered a lot in Rome, the quality of wine you served could raise or lower people's opinion of you. Serving poor wine to an honored guest was a serious mistake. On the other hand, offering famous wines like Falernian or Caecuban would boost your reputation as a generous and cultured host.

5.5.3 Everyday Wine Drinking

Wine was not just for the rich. Most Romans, including commoners, drank wine daily—though it was cheaper, lower-quality wine or sometimes watered down. In cities, small taverns or bars (called "tabernae" or "cauponae") sold wine to travelers, workers, and anyone wanting a quick drink. Wine also was sold in large markets, alongside grain, oil, and other staples.

Because water in urban areas could be unsafe, mixing some sour or cheap wine with water helped kill germs. Even children drank diluted wine at times, though not to get drunk. For many, wine was an ordinary part of meals, providing both calories and hydration.

5.6 Wine in Roman Religion and Myth

5.6.1 Bacchus and Religious Festivals

Romans had their own version of the Greek god Dionysus, called **Bacchus**. He was the god of wine, revelry, and freedom of expression. The **Bacchanalia** were festivals held in his honor, where participants drank wine, danced, and sometimes engaged in wild celebrations. Early on, these festivals were secret and associated with scandal. The Roman Senate even tried to limit them, fearing they could lead to political unrest. Over time, the worship of Bacchus became more regulated.

5.6.2 Sacrifices and Offerings

Romans also offered wine to other gods. During religious ceremonies, a priest or official poured out some wine as a libation on altars. They believed this act honored the gods and kept them pleased. Important events like treaties, military victories, or harvest festivals might include a ceremonial wine offering.

In household worship, known as the **Lares and Penates** cult (where families honored their household gods), wine was sometimes poured out on small shrines. This regular practice showed gratitude and asked for blessing over the family.

5.6.3 Myths and Beliefs

Roman myths about the origins of wine often mirrored Greek tales, since the Romans adopted much of Greek culture. Stories might describe how Bacchus traveled the earth teaching people to cultivate vines. While these myths provided spiritual meaning, wine also had a practical value in daily life. People loved to link their everyday wine-drinking to the divine gift from their gods.

5.7 Wine and Roman Law

5.7.1 Regulations and Taxes

Wine was big business in the Roman world. The government set taxes on vineyards, wine sales, and transport. This helped fund public works like roads, aqueducts, and city walls. In some periods, the state also regulated how many vines people could plant. Emperor Domitian, for example, supposedly tried to limit vineyard expansion in the provinces so that Italian wines wouldn't have too much competition. Later emperors relaxed these rules, allowing vineyards to grow again.

5.7.2 Quality Control

Romans disliked wine fraud, such as watering down or mixing cheap additives. Some laws punished tavern owners or merchants who cheated customers by selling fake or spoiled wine. While we do not have a detailed "wine inspection agency" as we might today, there were references in Roman literature to dishonest traders and the need to protect consumers.

5.7.3 Inheritance and Vineyard Ownership

In Roman society, landownership showed wealth and status. Vineyards were seen as valuable property because they could produce steady income. Roman laws on inheritance—like the famous "Twelve Tables" and later legal codes—set rules for how property, including vineyards, passed from one generation to another. Wealthy families often treasured their vineyards, keeping them for decades or even centuries.

5.8 The Economic Impact: Wine Trade Across the Empire

5.8.1 Wine as a Major Commodity

Along with olive oil and grain, wine was one of the most important goods traded throughout the Roman Empire. Merchant ships carried amphorae of wine from Italy to Gaul, Spain, Britain, Egypt, and beyond. Ports like Ostia (near Rome) or Puteoli (near Naples) bustled with activity, loading cargo for far-off provinces.

In return, Rome imported metals, timber, precious stones, and exotic goods from its colonies or allied states. This exchange tied the empire together and brought great wealth to merchant families who specialized in the wine business.

5.8.2 Amphora Stamps and Shipping

Many Roman amphorae had stamps or painted labels. The stamp might show the pottery workshop's name or symbol, and sometimes the vineyard or producer. This labeling helped people know if they were getting reputable wine. Over time, certain stamps became a mark of quality. Archaeologists today find these amphorae in shipwrecks and old warehouses, giving us a glimpse of ancient trade routes.

5.8.3 Influence on Local Economies

As wine drinking spread, local regions in Gaul, Spain, or North Africa began to produce their own wine. Soon, they were not only importing Italian wine but also exporting their own wines back to Rome or to other provinces. This meant that places outside Italy became famous for fine wines. Roman authors sometimes praised wines from Gaul or Hispania, proving how quickly the craft had spread.

Vineyards created jobs—from farmers to amphora makers to ship captains. Taverns and inns grew up along trade routes, catering to merchants and travelers who wanted wine after a long journey. All of this boosted local economies and made wine a key factor in the empire's prosperity.

5.9 Roman Innovations: Barrels and Beyond

5.9.1 Interaction with Other Cultures

As the Romans moved into regions north of the Alps—places inhabited by Celtic tribes—they encountered wooden barrels. The Celts had invented wooden barrels bound with iron or wooden hoops to store beer and other liquids. Romans recognized that these barrels could be useful for transporting wine over land, especially in areas where pottery amphorae might break easily.

Over time, Romans adopted barrel use, though amphorae remained popular for sea transport. This mixing of ideas showed how the empire blended different cultures to improve wine storage and shipping methods.

5.9.2 Wine Clubs and Social Gatherings

Romans also formed clubs or societies (collegia) that sometimes revolved around shared meals and wine drinking. People with common interests or jobs, like merchants, bakers, or soldiers, formed these groups for support and fellowship. At their gatherings, wine was consumed in moderation or for celebration. This was another example of how wine brought people together across social lines.

5.9.3 Techniques in Viticulture

Roman authors studied grape diseases and ways to prevent vine pests, such as insects or fungi. They knew about crop rotation, not always for vines but for other plants around them. By rotating what was grown in a region, the soil could maintain fertility. Though they lacked modern science, Romans were keen observers of nature, making changes when they saw patterns of success or failure in their vineyards.

5.10 Conclusion and Legacy of Roman Wine Culture

5.10.1 A Lasting Influence

The Romans took wine beyond its Greek origins, making it a central part of an entire empire. They spread grapes, winemaking techniques, and a love of wine to regions that later became modern-day France, Spain, Germany, and more. Their roads, storage methods, and laws all supported this massive wine market. By the time the Western Roman Empire began to fall in the 5th century CE, wine production was well rooted across Europe and parts of North Africa and the Middle East.

5.10.2 Preparing the Ground for the Future

After Rome's decline, new powers emerged. Yet the vineyards and wine traditions remained. As we move to the next chapter—about early Christian and monastic traditions—we will see how the legacy of Roman viticulture lived on through the Church and various monastic orders. The seeds the Romans planted helped shape the wine culture of medieval Europe and beyond.

CHAPTER 6

Wine in Early Christian and Monastic Traditions

6.1 Introduction

With the fall of the Western Roman Empire (commonly dated to 476 CE), Europe entered a period often called the Early Middle Ages. This was a time of shifting kingdoms, migrations, and the growth of Christianity as a powerful force. In this chapter, we will see how wine did not disappear with Rome. Instead, it found a new role in Christian worship and in the daily life of monks and other religious orders.

We will explore how monasteries became centers of grape growing and winemaking, ensuring that wine traditions survived even as many parts of Europe faced turmoil. We will also see how wine's religious meaning, especially in the Christian Eucharist (or Communion), guaranteed that grapes continued to be grown in large areas despite political changes.

6.2 The Role of Wine in Early Christianity

6.2.1 Biblical References

Wine appears throughout the Bible, both the Old Testament and the New Testament. Stories mention wine as a symbol of blessing, joy, and sometimes overindulgence. Jesus's first recorded miracle in the Gospel of John was turning water into wine at a wedding feast in Cana. This story gave wine a special place in Christian thought, suggesting it was more than just a casual drink.

Early Christians, many of whom lived in the former Roman Empire, continued to drink wine in daily life. But the most important use of wine for Christians was in the Eucharist—a ritual also called the Lord's Supper or Communion. In this practice, bread and wine recall the Last Supper of Jesus with his disciples, where he told them to remember him using these elements.

6.2.2 The Eucharist and Symbolism

During Communion, wine represents the blood of Christ. This made wine central to Christian worship. As Christianity spread across Europe, churches needed a steady supply of wine for these services. Even in regions less suited for grape growing, believers tried to establish vineyards or import wine from warmer areas.

This religious need ensured that vineyards did not vanish after Rome's collapse. Even small churches or local lords might maintain a patch of vines to meet sacramental requirements. Over time, the Church would become a major protector and promoter of viticulture, particularly through the work of monks in monasteries.

6.3 The Rise of Monasticism

6.3.1 What Is Monasticism?

Monasticism refers to the practice of withdrawing from the busy world to live a life of prayer, work, and community within a monastery (for monks) or a convent (for nuns). Early Christian monks first appeared in places like Egypt (the Desert Fathers), but the idea spread to Europe in later centuries.

Monasteries usually had to be self-sufficient. They farmed their own land, raised animals, and built their own structures. Because monks used wine for Communion, many monasteries planted vineyards so they could produce it themselves. Soon, wine became both a sacred element and an ordinary drink for daily use—since most communities in medieval times drank some form of alcoholic beverage rather than plain water.

6.3.2 St. Benedict and the Rule

A key figure in Western monasticism was **St. Benedict of Nursia** (480–547 CE). He wrote the "Rule of St. Benedict," a guide for monastic life that became standard in many European monasteries. The Rule encouraged a balanced life of prayer, study, and manual labor.

Though Benedict's Rule does not go into deep detail about wine production, it does mention the allowance of wine for monks in moderation, recognizing that harsh climates or limited water supply often made wine a more practical drink. Over time, many Benedictine monasteries in Italy, France, Germany, and other lands established vineyards, developing high-quality winemaking skills.

6.3.3 Monastic Work and Vines

Monks were known for their discipline and careful record-keeping. They applied this focus to vineyard management. They observed which grapes grew best, how to prune vines properly, and the best time to harvest. They also improved wine cellars, sometimes building underground storage areas to keep the temperature stable.

Because monasteries often exchanged knowledge with each other, ideas about grape growing and winemaking spread from one region to another. Over the centuries, certain monasteries became famous for their wine, selling or trading surplus to local people and travelers. This income helped the monasteries support their charitable works, libraries, and guesthouses.

6.4 Monastic Vineyards Across Europe

6.4.1 France: Burgundy and Beyond

France eventually became one of the world's best-known wine regions, and monasteries played a huge part in that story. Around the 6th to 9th centuries, monastic communities, such as the Benedictines and later the Cistercians, cleared land for vines and recorded detailed observations of soil and climate. In Burgundy, for instance, monks identified small plots (later called "climats" or "terroirs") that produced wines with distinct flavors.

By studying different fields year after year, these monks discovered that vines grown on certain slopes gave better-quality grapes. Over time, they separated these slopes into specific vineyards, a practice that lives on in modern French wine regulations (though we are not focusing on modern times, it is important to note the historical roots).

6.4.2 Germany: Along the Rhine

Christian monasteries near the Rhine River in Germany also cultivated vines. Despite the cooler climate, certain river valleys provided the right conditions for grapes. Monks found that steep slopes facing the sun and reflecting light from the river produced grapes that could ripen enough for wine.

They experimented with grape types suited to cooler regions, paving the way for a long tradition of German wine. Though the earliest records may be sparse, we do know that these religious houses managed to sustain vineyards in lands that the Romans had once cultivated but which needed careful attention in the post-Roman era.

6.4.3 Iberian Peninsula and Other Areas

In the regions of modern Spain and Portugal (once part of the Roman provinces like Hispania and Lusitania), the Church also preserved wine culture. After the collapse of Roman rule, various kingdoms and cultures took shape. Yet monasteries remained stable centers of learning, worship, and wine production. They passed on vine-growing skills from one generation of monks to the next.

Similar patterns appeared in parts of Italy, where ancient Roman vineyards continued under the watchful eyes of monastic communities. Even in places like England, monks tried cultivating vines near monasteries, though the cooler, damp climate made successful viticulture more difficult.

6.5 Wine Production in Monasteries

6.5.1 Tools and Techniques

Monastic wine production often resembled Roman or Greek methods but with small improvements. Monks used wooden presses or stone presses to crush grapes. They stored the juice in barrels or large clay vats, depending on local traditions. Over time, they became more skilled at controlling fermentation temperatures—sometimes by placing barrels in cool cellars or caves.

Monasteries typically documented their work meticulously. They might note the date of planting new vines, the weather during the growing season, and the day they began harvesting. These records helped them see patterns and refine their practices. As literacy was more common among monks than in the general population, monasteries became the keepers of agricultural science, including viticulture.

6.5.2 Labor and Community

Monks followed a daily schedule of prayer, meals, and work. Tending vineyards fit neatly into this routine. During harvest season, the entire community (including lay brothers or hired laborers) would gather grapes quickly to avoid rot or damage. Once the grapes were pressed, monks cared for the wine in the cellar, checking it as it fermented and racking it off the lees (sediments) to improve clarity.

Because monasteries also provided hospitality to travelers, pilgrims, and church officials, they needed a consistent supply of wine. Serving guests a cup of local wine was a sign of welcome. It also showcased the monastery's skill and resources, often attracting donations or respect from visitors.

6.5.3 Quality and Reputation

Some monasteries became famous for producing fine wines. Church leaders, nobles, and even kings took notice. They might grant more land to a successful monastery so it could expand production. The monastery's wine could then be served at royal courts or important church gatherings.

In places like Cluny or Cîteaux (major monastic centers in medieval France), the reputation for high-quality wine spread far and wide. These monastic wines often fetched good prices, providing income that allowed the communities to fund new building projects, care for the poor, and copy manuscripts in their scriptoria (writing rooms).

6.6 The Christianization of Wine Culture

6.6.1 Missionaries and New Vines

As Christianity spread beyond the old Roman frontiers, missionaries carried their faith to new lands in Central and Northern Europe. Along with the Gospel, they brought knowledge of grape growing and wine production. When they established monasteries in these regions, they sometimes planted vineyards if the climate allowed. If it was too cold for vines, they often imported wine for the Eucharist from warmer areas.

This means that the geographic reach of wine expanded wherever monasteries had a foothold. Even if a region did not become a major wine producer, the presence of a monastery could introduce local people to vines, either as laborers or as buyers of grapes. Over the centuries, some of these vines took root and adapted to new climates, slowly extending Europe's wine belt northward and eastward.

6.6.2 Feasts and Fasts

The Church calendar featured many feast days, celebrating saints and holy events. On these days, monasteries might share extra wine with the community, along with special foods. Conversely, there were also fasting periods, like Lent, when Christians practiced abstinence from certain foods or drinks. However, complete abstinence from wine was not always required, especially if wine was seen as part of daily sustenance or a necessary liquid in areas with poor water quality.

Balancing feasts and fasts allowed monks to show moderation. They could enjoy wine in a community setting when the calendar permitted, but also demonstrate self-discipline when the rules called for simpler meals.

6.6.3 Wine as a Symbol of Conversion

In some lands, local pagan customs involved alcoholic drinks made from grains or honey (like beer or mead). When the Church arrived, they promoted wine in Christian rituals. Over time, many communities accepted wine as a sacred drink. This shift did not always replace older traditions entirely—beer and mead continued to be popular in northern regions—but it ensured wine's special place in church ceremonies.

6.7 Challenges and Changes in the Early Middle Ages

6.7.1 Invasions and Instability

After Rome fell, various groups—like the Goths, Vandals, Lombards, and later the Vikings—moved across Europe. Some areas suffered war and devastation. Vineyards were abandoned or destroyed in certain regions, especially if armies marched through them. However, the monasteries, often respected as holy places, could survive or rebuild more easily. This allowed them to continue preserving wine-growing knowledge.

In some cases, new rulers found that supporting monasteries brought stability and organization to their lands. The monasteries, in turn, kept planting vines and making wine, since it was essential to worship and daily nutrition.

6.7.2 The Influence of Local Lords

Feudalism shaped much of early medieval Europe. Local lords controlled land and owed loyalty to a king or higher noble. Monasteries could own land too, given as a gift by a king or noble seeking spiritual favor. With these land grants, monasteries had the freedom to farm grapes without heavy interference. But sometimes they had to share a portion of their wine or profits with their feudal lord.

If a monastery's wine was famous or profitable, nearby lords might encourage expansion or protect the monastery from raids. This mutual benefit helped keep vineyards alive, even in regions that faced political struggles.

6.7.3 Maintaining Roman Traditions

Monks inherited many Roman farming techniques. They used Roman roads, aqueducts, and cellar designs whenever possible. For example, if a monastery was built near an old Roman villa with a pre-existing wine press, they might restore and use it. They read whatever Latin manuscripts they could find—though many were lost in the chaotic years after the empire fell.

By passing on Roman and early Christian agricultural practices, monks formed a link between the ancient world and the emerging medieval order. Even as new kingdoms replaced old Roman provinces, the art of wine production carried on.

6.8 Learning, Writing, and Wine

6.8.1 Scriptoriums and Books

Monasteries did more than produce wine. They were centers of learning. Monks copied biblical texts, classical works, and practical guides on farming. Some of these writings included sections about viticulture or references to Roman authors like Columella. In this way, knowledge of wine cultivation survived in handwritten manuscripts.

When traveling monks visited other monasteries, they sometimes brought copies of these texts or shared ideas they had learned. This network of knowledge exchange ensured that improvements in wine production could spread, even without a centralized empire like Rome.

6.8.2 Practical Skills

Because many medieval people could not read or write, monastic leaders often taught by example. Novice monks learned to care for vineyards from older monks who had decades of experience. This hands-on method passed down vital techniques, ensuring that each new generation knew when to prune, how to fight off pests, and the best way to store wine.

Laypeople working for the monastery or living nearby might also learn these skills, applying them to their small farms. In this way, the entire region benefited from the monastic dedication to wine.

6.9 Trade and Pilgrimage

6.9.1 Selling Monastic Wine

While some monasteries produced just enough wine for their needs, others made surplus. They sold this extra wine in local markets or to traveling merchants. Over time, certain monastic wines became known for their quality. They might reach distant towns, especially if the monastery was near a river or a trade route.

Profits from wine sales helped monasteries maintain their buildings, feed the poor, and welcome pilgrims. It also gave them funds to invest in better vineyard equipment, leading to an ongoing cycle of improvement.

6.9.2 Pilgrimage Routes

During the Middle Ages, pilgrimage was a common act of devotion. People traveled long distances to visit holy sites, such as Rome, Jerusalem, or the shrine of St. James at Santiago de Compostela. On these journeys, pilgrims often passed through regions famous for wine or stayed at monasteries for lodging.

Monasteries would offer pilgrims a place to sleep and sometimes a cup of local wine to warm them. Pilgrims might carry home stories of the fine wines they tasted, indirectly marketing those wines to the pilgrim's hometown. This helped spread the reputation of certain wine-producing monasteries even further.

6.10 Conclusion: Monastic Foundations for Wine's Future

6.10.1 Preserving Through Hard Times

During the early medieval period, Europe was far from peaceful or united. Yet, amid invasions, power struggles, and shifting kingdoms, the Church and its monasteries provided continuity. Monastic communities kept vineyards alive and carefully honed their winemaking craft. Their devotion to the Eucharist meant wine had to remain part of Christian life, regardless of outside turmoil.

6.10.2 Seeds of Regional Styles

In many areas, monks laid the groundwork for what would become famous wine regions in later centuries. They identified the best slopes, soils, and grape varieties for each locale, creating a tradition of terroir (the idea that the land gives unique character to wine). As new monastic orders formed and older ones spread, they took these practices with them.

CHAPTER 7

Wine in the Medieval Period

7.1 Introduction

The medieval period in Europe (roughly from the 5th century to the 15th century) was a time of great change. After the collapse of the Western Roman Empire, new kingdoms emerged. Feudalism took hold, with kings, nobles, knights, and peasants filling different roles in society. The Church also gained power, and monasteries continued to be centers of learning and agriculture.

During this long era, wine remained important in daily life, religion, and trade. People in regions suited for viticulture—like parts of France, Germany, Italy, and Spain—expanded vineyards. Feudal lords prized high-quality wine, while farmers and townspeople drank cheaper versions. In this chapter, we will see how wine influenced medieval society, from noble feasts to peasant meals. We will also explore how trade routes grew, spreading different wine styles across Europe. By the end, you will have a clear picture of how wine evolved as an economic and cultural force in the medieval world.

7.2 Feudal Society and Wine

7.2.1 Feudalism and Land Ownership

Medieval Europe ran on a system called **feudalism**, where land was the main source of wealth. Kings granted large areas of land (fiefs) to powerful nobles or lords. In return, these lords provided military support to the king. Peasants (sometimes called serfs) worked the land, giving part of their harvest to the lord.

Within this system, vineyards were prime assets. A vineyard could generate valuable wine, which the lord could either drink, sell, or use as rent payment. Sometimes, peasants grew grapes on small plots, handing over a portion of their wine or grapes to fulfill their obligations. This arrangement helped keep vineyards in use despite political unrest. Even in times of war, both lords and peasants had reasons to protect their vines.

7.2.2 Nobility and the Demand for Fine Wine

Wealthy nobles and knights loved hosting banquets in their castles or manor houses. Wine was central to these feasts, served alongside roasted meats, fresh bread, and sweet pastries. Owning a private vineyard or receiving shipments of fine wine from famous wine regions boosted a noble's reputation.

Sometimes, nobles competed to see who could serve the best or rarest wine at special events. Wine also acted as a diplomatic gift between kingdoms or powerful families. A noble might send barrels of good wine to another lord as a gesture of friendship (or to secure favor). This practice kept the idea of quality wine alive across different feudal territories.

7.2.3 Peasants and Everyday Wine

While peasants worked the land, their daily wine was usually simpler and cheaper. It might be a weak, quickly fermented drink that did not keep for long. People often mixed wine with water, just as in earlier eras, to stretch it out. In many rural areas, water sources were not always safe, so lightly fermented beverages were safer to drink. Even children sometimes drank watered-down wine because it was less risky than unclean water.

If a peasant family lived near a monastery or a large vineyard, they might help harvest grapes or press them for wages or for a share of the wine. Small allowances of wine could also be part of their payment in kind (meaning payment through goods rather than money). This arrangement ensured that even poorer communities had some access to wine, though usually not the fine vintages enjoyed by the upper classes.

7.3 Influence of the Church and Monasteries

7.3.1 Continuing the Monastic Tradition

As we saw in earlier chapters, monasteries were key to preserving wine production after the Roman Empire's fall. They carried on Roman knowledge about pruning, harvesting, and fermentation. In the medieval era, this work continued to grow. Certain monastic orders, like the Benedictines and Cistercians, expanded their networks of abbeys across Europe, often focusing on high-quality vineyard management.

These monasteries held large tracts of land, granted to them by nobles or kings who wished to support the Church. Monks cultivated grapevines, made wine for religious ceremonies (the Eucharist), and often sold surplus wine to local townspeople. Some monasteries became rich from wine trade, reinvesting earnings into more land and better cellars.

7.3.2 Wine for Religious Ceremonies

Wine was central in Christian worship, symbolizing the blood of Christ during the Eucharist. Every church, from grand cathedrals to small chapels, needed a regular supply. If a church lacked vines, it had to buy wine, sometimes transported from far away. This steady demand kept vineyards profitable.

Moreover, feast days and other religious celebrations in medieval Europe were common. On these occasions, churches or local lords might offer communal meals or free cups of wine, strengthening ties within the community. Weddings, baptisms, and festivals often took place under Church supervision, ensuring that wine had a role in nearly every major life event.

7.3.3 Monastic Innovation and Record Keeping

Monks were among the few literate groups in the early Middle Ages. They wrote down which grape varieties thrived in certain soils and how different weather patterns affected the harvest. Over time, these records helped improve wine quality. By comparing notes, monasteries discovered that planting on certain hillsides produced grapes with better flavor. They also refined fermentation methods, sometimes reusing yeast from one batch to the next to maintain consistent results.

In regions like Burgundy (France) or the Rhine Valley (Germany), monks divided vineyards into specific sections, noting differences in taste. These early observations laid the groundwork for the concept of "terroir," or the idea that unique soils and climates create unique wine characters. Though the term "terroir" was not used exactly like we do today, the medieval monks recognized that each vineyard had its own special quality.

7.4 Wine Trade and Growing Markets

7.4.1 Medieval Trade Routes

Trade in medieval Europe developed along rivers, over land routes, and via the sea. Towns grew around major roads or river crossings, and merchants formed guilds to protect their interests. Wine was one of the main goods traded. Certain regions became famous for exporting wine to distant markets:

- **Southwestern France (Bordeaux region)**: Shipped wine to England and Northern Europe.
- **Rhine Valley (Germany)**: Sent white wines downstream or by land to many German towns and beyond.
- **Northern Italy (like Tuscany)**: Produced wines that were traded throughout the Italian peninsula and beyond.

Ships carried barrels or casks of wine—an improvement over the older amphorae method—for easier transport and loading. Smaller kegs were loaded onto carts and hauled to fairs in distant towns. Cities like Venice, Genoa, and Bruges served as major trading hubs, dealing in wine among other goods.

7.4.2 Wine Fairs

In medieval Europe, large fairs were held in certain towns, sometimes lasting for weeks. Merchants arrived from far away to sell cloth, spices, metals, and wine. The **Champagne Fairs** in northern France are a famous example. These fairs offered an ideal place for vineyard owners, monasteries, and middlemen to connect with buyers. By showcasing their wines, they could attract wealthy nobles, innkeepers, or even foreign traders who wanted to buy in bulk and transport the wine back home.

7.4.3 Rise of Wine Guilds

To protect their trade, wine merchants and vintners (winegrowers) formed **guilds**. A guild set rules on prices, quality, and how apprentices could learn the trade. Guild members took pride in their craft, aiming to ensure that buyers received genuine, unspoiled wine. If a merchant diluted wine or sold a lower-quality product than promised, the guild could punish or ban him.

These guilds helped maintain consistent standards. Over time, this also boosted the reputation of certain wine regions. If a buyer trusted the local guild, they were more likely to buy wine from that place, knowing it had passed inspections. This system laid an early foundation for brand identity and quality control, even though it was far simpler than today's regulations.

7.5 Changes in Grape Varieties and Techniques

7.5.1 Adapting to Cooler Climates

After the so-called "Medieval Warm Period" (roughly 10th to 13th centuries), Europe experienced shifts in climate that occasionally made grape-growing difficult in cooler areas. Some regions that once had thriving vines found yields dropping. In response, growers tried different grape varieties that were more tolerant of cooler or wetter conditions.

In places like the southern half of England, there was a small but real tradition of viticulture, started in Roman times and continued by monasteries. Gradually, as temperatures changed, these vineyards struggled. Still, the knowledge about how to handle cooler climates spread to areas like the Rhine or Mosel valleys in Germany, reinforcing new grape choices suited to crisp, less sunny weather.

7.5.2 Advances in Barrel Making

During the medieval period, wooden barrels replaced many clay jars for shipping wine. Skilled coopers (barrel makers) became essential to the wine trade. They crafted barrels from oak staves held together by metal hoops. Barrels were easier to stack in cellars and simpler to roll onto ships. They also had an impact on the wine's taste, as oak can give subtle flavors.

While the Romans had experimented with wooden barrels—adopting the idea from Celtic tribes—medieval coopers refined the craft. They realized that certain types of wood and certain ways of charring or toasting the inside of a barrel could affect the wine's aroma. However, these refinements were still in their early stages, and detailed knowledge of oak aging would develop more fully in later centuries.

7.5.3 Increased Use of Sulfur

Some medieval winemakers discovered that burning sulfur inside a barrel before filling it with wine could help preserve freshness and prevent spoilage. This practice likely came from trial and error, as they noticed that wine stored in sulfur-treated barrels stayed more stable. Early references to sulfur use appear in texts about preserving wine during long journeys. Over time, this method spread among serious vintners, though it was still not universally applied.

7.6 Social Customs and Beliefs About Wine

7.6.1 Manners and Feasting

Medieval feasts, especially in noble circles, were theatrical affairs with music, dancing, and large platters of food. Wine flowed freely, served in metal or pottery cups. Because table manners were evolving during this period, hosts and guests followed certain rules: for example, you might wait for a toast from the lord of the house before drinking. People also learned not to gulp wine too quickly or they risked losing respect.

Courtiers (people at a royal or noble court) sometimes played drinking games or tested each other's ability to recite poetry or tell stories while sipping wine. Troubadours and minstrels performed songs celebrating knights and ladies, and wine was part of the lively atmosphere.

7.6.2 Attitudes Toward Drunkenness

While wine was widely consumed, extreme drunkenness was not always admired. Church leaders and moralists wrote sermons against overindulgence. They viewed drunkenness as a sin or a gateway to other sins. Still, in many rural communities, wine was considered a normal part of life. The difference lay in how much one drank and on what occasions.

In some medieval tales, knights or peasants who got too drunk were shown as foolish, risking fights or ridicule. This suggests that, although wine was central to social events, there was also an understanding that it should be used responsibly. Monks, for instance, were advised to keep moderation at meal times, though some accounts say they occasionally enjoyed quite a bit of wine after long days of work!

7.6.3 Symbolic Role in Literature

Medieval literature often used wine as a symbol of celebration, fertility, or spiritual significance. In the **Arthurian legends**, feasts at Camelot included wine, showcasing the kingdom's prosperity. Poets sang about how wine could bring warmth and fellowship, yet they also warned of its power to cause troubles if handled poorly.

As the Middle Ages progressed, wine became linked with certain saints or local legends. For instance, St. Urban was sometimes considered a protector of vineyards in parts of Europe. People prayed to him for good weather and bountiful harvests. These beliefs show how strongly wine had become woven into the spiritual and cultural fabric of medieval life.

7.7 Major Wine Regions of the Medieval Era

7.7.1 France

France was a leading producer in the medieval period. Regions like Bordeaux exported wine to England, particularly after the marriage of Eleanor of Aquitaine to King Henry II of England in the mid-12th century. This political link encouraged huge wine shipments across the Channel. Burgundy and the Champagne region also refined their vineyard practices, largely under monastic guidance.

7.7.2 The Holy Roman Empire (Germany and Surrounding Areas)

Along the Rhine and Mosel rivers, vineyards multiplied. Monasteries and noble estates planted vines on steep slopes overlooking the water. White grapes thrived, producing lighter, aromatic wines. Towns like Mainz, Worms, and Trier became centers of wine trade. River barges carried wine downstream, connecting these regions to the North Sea.

7.7.3 Italy

Italy, once the heart of Roman wine culture, continued its strong tradition. Cities like Florence, Siena, and Venice grew in wealth, and wine from Tuscany, Umbria, and other regions found local and foreign buyers. The Pope's residence in Rome ensured a steady demand for church wine, while republics like Venice shipped Italian wine across the Mediterranean.

7.7.4 Spain

In medieval Spain, the Reconquista (the Christian effort to reclaim land from Muslim rulers) shaped wine production. In Christian-controlled areas, monasteries and local farmers tended vineyards. However, in territories under Muslim rule, wine production faced challenges because Islam generally prohibits alcohol. Still, many Jewish and Christian communities in those regions kept small vineyards, and the local rulers often tolerated wine for non-Muslim inhabitants.

7.8 The Later Middle Ages: Challenges and Shifts

7.8.1 The Black Death

The **Black Death** (mid-14th century) was a devastating plague that killed a large part of Europe's population. This tragedy had many social and economic effects, including on wine. With fewer workers available to tend the vines, some vineyards were abandoned or scaled back. Wages went up for those who survived because labor was in high demand. Some smaller farms combined into bigger estates, changing how vineyards were managed.

However, the reduced population also meant lower overall demand for wine. Prices could fluctuate wildly. In some regions, wealthy landowners kept their vineyards going by paying higher wages, while poorer growers struggled. Over time, the wine trade recovered, but the Black Death left deep marks on medieval society.

7.8.2 Political Conflicts

Medieval Europe saw many wars, such as the **Hundred Years' War** between England and France (1337–1453). Regions like Bordeaux, which depended on shipping wine to England, were caught in the conflict. When the English lost territories in France, wine exports changed dramatically. Some areas faced occupation, vineyards were sometimes destroyed, and trade routes became dangerous.

Still, wine remained a cherished commodity. Armies marching through a region might loot wine cellars or demand supplies from local farmers. Towns that survived tried to rebuild quickly, knowing wine was a major source of income and essential for daily life. This mix of war and rebuilding happened repeatedly in parts of medieval Europe, testing the resilience of wine culture.

7.8.3 New Commercial Centers

By the 14th and 15th centuries, certain cities like Bruges, Ghent, and Lübeck became major trading centers in northern Europe.

Merchants there bought wine from southern regions and sold it across the Baltic Sea area. This trade created a wide network where Spanish, French, and German wines reached places as far north as Scandinavia or as far east as Poland.

In the Italian city-states, commerce grew as well. Venice dominated sea trade, bringing wines from the eastern Mediterranean or shipping local wines out. Banking families like the Medici in Florence accumulated wealth partly from trade (including wine). All these developments laid the groundwork for an even bigger surge in trade and exploration that would come with the Renaissance and Age of Exploration.

7.9 Cultural Exchange and Influence

7.9.1 Contacts with the Islamic World

Despite religious differences, Europe's contact with the Islamic world also affected wine production. While most Muslim rulers forbid drinking wine in public, some kept private vineyards or allowed Christian and Jewish minorities to produce wine. Trade routes through the Mediterranean and the Middle East often exchanged ideas and farming practices.

During the Crusades (1096–late 1200s), knights traveling to the Holy Land encountered new spices, fruits, and possibly different approaches to agriculture. They sometimes brought these ideas back to Europe, experimenting with new ways of flavoring or preserving wine.

7.9.2 Influence on Art and Music

In medieval art, wine frequently appeared in religious paintings, illustrating biblical scenes or saints. Artists also depicted vineyard labor in the margins of illuminated manuscripts, showing peasants harvesting grapes or stomping them. Musicians wrote songs praising wine, feasting, and fellowship. These cultural expressions underscored wine's deep roots in medieval life, from everyday labor to spiritual imagery.

7.10 Transition to the Renaissance

7.10.1 The Dawn of a New Era

By the late Middle Ages, Europe was changing. Population began to recover from plagues and wars. Cities were growing, trade was expanding, and a new interest in classical learning was emerging—an interest that would develop into the **Renaissance**. While the Renaissance is often associated with art, science, and literature, it also brought changes to agriculture and trade, including wine.

7.10.2 Looking Ahead

In the following chapter, we will explore how wine found new opportunities as maritime exploration increased and wealthy patrons supported arts and culture. New merchant classes arose, investing in bigger wine trade operations. More efficient ships and better navigation methods helped European powers move wine around the world, though we will limit our focus to times before modern history.

CHAPTER 8

Renaissance Europe and the Rise of Wine Trade

8.1 Introduction

The Renaissance (which began in parts of Europe around the 14th century and lasted into the 17th century, depending on the region) was a time of renewed interest in art, science, philosophy, and classical learning. It started in Italy and spread across the continent. This cultural rebirth also affected agriculture, commerce, and social structures.

New trade networks emerged as merchant families and city-states became wealthier. Explorers like Vasco da Gama and Christopher Columbus (though we will not dive deep into their voyages, as that belongs more to the Age of Exploration in Chapter 9) set the stage for global connections. Meanwhile, Europe itself saw an expansion of vineyards, improvements in wine-making techniques, and an ever-growing thirst for quality wines among both nobles and the rising middle class.

In this chapter, we will see how the Renaissance spirit shaped wine culture. We will focus on how improved economic conditions and greater curiosity about the world led to new trade deals. We will also explore how major Renaissance cities became hubs for wine distribution, how new classes of society began drinking wine more regularly, and how knowledge about grape growing continued to evolve.

8.2 The Changing Social Landscape

8.2.1 The Rise of a Wealthy Merchant Class

During the Middle Ages, land-owning nobles and the Church held much of the power. In the Renaissance, however, a wealthy merchant class rose in importance. Families like the Medici in Florence gained influence by banking, trading, and financing major art projects. These merchants saw business opportunities in goods like textiles, spices, and—of course—wine.

Unlike feudal lords, merchant families did not always rely on farmland for their wealth. They used profits from trade to invest in vineyards or to import the best wines. They served fine wines at lavish banquets to display their status. As more merchants became wealthy, the demand for premium wine grew, driving vineyards to produce higher-quality products rather than just large quantities.

8.2.2 Urban Growth and Wine Demand

Renaissance Europe saw the growth of cities: Florence, Venice, Milan, and Rome in Italy; Brussels and Antwerp in the Low Countries; and major centers in France, Spain, Germany, and England. Urban populations demanded food and drink from the countryside. Wine, being both a pleasurable drink and safer than plain water, became a staple in many city taverns and inns.

City dwellers, from shopkeepers to artisans, found ways to buy modest-quality wine. Over time, this created a broader market than in the Middle Ages, when good wine was often limited to nobles and clerics. More taverns opened to meet the growing demand, offering wines from nearby regions or from famous producing areas abroad.

8.2.3 The Courtly and Intellectual Elite

Alongside merchants, Renaissance courts—run by dukes, princes, or kings—hosted intellectuals and artists. Patrons often sponsored painters like Leonardo da Vinci or Michelangelo, as well as writers and philosophers. These courts valued luxurious living, which included fine wines at feasts and gatherings.

In these refined circles, wine was not just consumed for taste but also discussed in a cultured way. Poets might dedicate verses to a particular vintage. Scholars debated the health benefits or potential risks of wine. This intellectual interest led some thinkers to study grape cultivation and the science behind fermentation, adding a scholarly aspect to winemaking.

8.3 Agricultural Advances in the Renaissance

8.3.1 Rediscovery of Classical Texts

One hallmark of the Renaissance was the rediscovery of Greek and Roman writings. Scholars translated ancient texts about farming, including works by Roman authors like Columella and Cato. These texts contained advice on vineyard management and wine production that had been partly forgotten or preserved only in monasteries.

By studying these writings, Renaissance farmers and landowners learned new (or rather old) techniques about pruning, soil care, and pest control. This exchange of knowledge sometimes led to experiments in the vineyards, with landowners testing different methods to improve grape quality.

8.3.2 Crop Rotation and Land Management

The Renaissance also saw developments in general agriculture. Some estates tried more efficient **crop rotation**, planting different crops each season to keep the soil rich. While not all land was suited for vines, having a stronger overall farming system allowed wealthier landowners to invest more in specialized crops like grapes.

Irrigation channels or improved drainage methods further helped certain vineyards flourish. In regions with heavier rainfall, farmers learned to direct excess water away from the vines. In drier areas, landowners built small canals or cisterns to store water for the hottest months. These improvements made vineyards more resilient in changing weather conditions.

8.3.3 Tools and Technology

Metal tools became sturdier and more widespread. Shears, spades, and plows of better quality allowed vineyard workers to maintain vines with greater ease. Barrels made from carefully selected oak advanced beyond the medieval style, as coopers fine-tuned barrel shapes and sealing methods. Some Renaissance scholars even wrote about the chemistry of wine spoilage, hinting at early scientific approaches to controlling fermentation.

8.4 Commerce and Wine Distribution

8.4.1 Expansion of Maritime Trade

During the Renaissance, maritime trade grew rapidly. Italian city-states like Venice and Genoa built strong navies and merchant fleets. Portugal and Spain explored the Atlantic, while England and the Netherlands also developed seafaring economies. Although the primary focus of exploration involved spices, gold, and new trade routes, wine was part of the broader commercial activity.

For instance, Genoese and Venetian traders sailed the Mediterranean, carrying wine from southern Europe to ports in the East. They returned with goods like silk, spices, and precious metals. In the west, ports like Lisbon in Portugal and Seville in Spain also exported local wines overseas, though much of that trade expanded more significantly in the Age of Exploration.

8.4.2 Overland Routes and Regional Fairs

Land routes improved as many Renaissance rulers invested in roads to boost commerce. Inns and waystations popped up, offering wine to travelers and merchants. Large fairs continued to be a central meeting point for buyers and sellers. Regions like Champagne in France or certain German towns had seasonal fairs where merchants could make deals for wines from Burgundy, the Rhineland, or even farther away.

Having multiple routes to sell wine—both overland and by sea—encouraged vineyard owners to produce more, knowing they had ways to reach customers beyond their immediate area. This boosted local economies and allowed certain wine regions to specialize in distinctive styles or grape varieties, confident they could find buyers in distant markets.

8.4.3 Emerging Wine Markets Beyond Europe

While the bulk of Renaissance wine trade happened within Europe, glimpses of future global markets began. Diplomatic envoys from the Ottoman Empire or North Africa might sample European wines (though these regions largely followed Islamic laws, which typically forbade alcohol). Some rare shipments of European wine may have reached places like the Indian coast through indirect trade routes. These were small-scale at the time, but they foreshadowed the eventual worldwide spread of wine.

8.5 Influence of Art and Learning on Wine

8.5.1 Wine in Renaissance Art

Renaissance artists, funded by wealthy patrons, often included scenes of everyday life in their paintings. Depictions of grape harvests or wine drinking appeared in frescoes or panel paintings.

Religious art still showed biblical wine imagery, such as the Wedding at Cana or the Last Supper. Meanwhile, secular paintings might portray banquet scenes where noblemen and women savor fine wines in splendid dining halls.

Sometimes, an artist would embed hidden symbolism in these scenes. A wine jug might symbolize hospitality or abundance, while a half-empty cup could hint at the fleeting nature of life. These layered meanings showed how deeply wine had woven itself into Renaissance culture—both as a real beverage and a powerful symbol.

8.5.2 Scientific Observation and Books

The Renaissance spirit of inquiry prompted more written works about the natural world, including plants, grapes, and fermentation. Scholars tried to categorize grape varieties, describing their appearance and taste. While they did not fully understand yeast or bacteria, they realized that cleanliness in wine storage and controlling air contact mattered for wine quality.

Some landowners sponsored treatises on agriculture, which included sections on viticulture. These books spread from Italy to France, Spain, and other parts of Europe, gradually improving wine techniques. By combining ancient knowledge from Roman texts with current observations, Renaissance writers laid the groundwork for more advanced wine science in later centuries.

8.5.3 Philosophical and Cultural Debates

Humanist writers of the Renaissance sometimes discussed wine's role in society. Some praised it as a gift from God, bringing joy and friendship. Others warned against the moral dangers of excess. These debates echoed those of the medieval Church but took on a more philosophical tone, reflecting the Renaissance's broader interest in human behavior, virtue, and vice.

8.6 Notable Wine Regions During the Renaissance

8.6.1 Italy: Tuscany and Beyond

Italy remained a patchwork of city-states—Milan, Florence, Venice, Naples, and the Papal States. Tuscany, in particular, gained a name for strong, earthy reds. The ruling Medici family in Florence supported arts and scholarship, hosting many feasts with local wines. The hills around Florence and Siena saw expanded vineyards, with landowners competing to produce better vintages. In Rome, the Papal Court required vast amounts of wine for religious rituals and entertaining guests from around Europe.

8.6.2 France: Burgundy, Champagne, Bordeaux

France during the Renaissance was ruled by monarchs like Francis I (early 16th century). Although the feudal system was changing, many large estates remained. Burgundy refined its vineyards, where monastic knowledge intersected with noble patronage. Champagne, known for lighter wines that sometimes developed a bit of sparkle (though true sparkling wine had not fully emerged yet), gained recognition for its fresh taste. Bordeaux continued shipping wine, especially to England and the Low Countries, building on centuries of trade.

8.6.3 Iberian Peninsula: Spain and Portugal

Spain saw the marriage of Isabella of Castile and Ferdinand of Aragon (late 15th century), uniting major Spanish kingdoms. They sponsored voyages that led to the "discovery" of new lands (though we leave fuller exploration details to the next chapter). Spanish regions like La Rioja and Ribera del Duero quietly improved their wines, which were consumed domestically and sometimes exported.

Portugal, meanwhile, had strong ties with England, sending wines through Atlantic ports. The city of Porto, near the Douro Valley, was already shipping wine, though "Port wine" in its famous fortified style would develop more fully in later centuries. Still, the seeds of that tradition were being planted in the Renaissance.

8.6.4 The Holy Roman Empire and Beyond

Much of Central Europe was part of the Holy Roman Empire. German states along the Rhine and Mosel built on the medieval legacy of white wine production. Towns like Würzburg, Frankfurt, and Cologne imported and exported wine. Farther east, in regions like Bohemia or Poland, wine drinking was more common among nobles and city elites, who often imported casks from western vineyards. Some local vineyards existed in Hungary or Transylvania, producing distinctive wines that occasionally reached western markets.

8.7 Social Gatherings and Banquets

8.7.1 Renaissance Banquet Culture

Renaissance banquets could be even more extravagant than medieval feasts. The wealthy class wanted to display their power, sophistication, and education. Large tables held multiple courses of meats, pastries, sugared fruits, and spiced dishes. Wine accompanied each course. Skilled wine stewards (known in some places as "cupbearers") selected different wines to match the food, an early form of pairing.

Entertainment included musicians, dancers, poetry readings, or even small theatrical performances. The host often aimed to impress guests with variety, serving sweet wines at the end of the meal or after dessert. Guests would lounge on cushions or sit on carved wooden chairs, discussing art and philosophy.

8.7.2 Taverns and Wine Shops

For common people, taverns and wine shops offered simpler enjoyment. City neighborhoods often had small establishments where artisans, minor merchants, and travelers could buy a cup of wine. Tavern keepers sometimes specialized in wines from a particular region, advertising with signs or special symbols. People also gathered to talk politics, hear local news, and socialize.

In some cities, local governments regulated taverns, setting rules on prices and behavior. If fights broke out or if the wine was watered down too much, authorities could shut a tavern down. Despite these controls, taverns were a major part of everyday life, bridging the gap between the upper-class feasts and ordinary drinking needs.

8.8 Challenges in Renaissance Wine Production

8.8.1 War and Territorial Disputes

Like the Middle Ages, the Renaissance period had its share of conflicts. Italy, for instance, saw wars between city-states and invasions by France or Spain. Vineyards in contested regions could be destroyed or heavily taxed to fund military campaigns. Peasants sometimes fled their lands, leaving grapes untended. When peace returned, landowners had to rebuild, replant, or hire new workers.

8.8.2 Climate Variations

Europe's climate continued to fluctuate, with cold snaps or storms that ruined harvests. This was still centuries before modern understanding of weather patterns, so farmers relied on observation and local wisdom. A few years of bad weather could devastate a vineyard, leading to poor yields and financial strain. Wealthier estates with multiple farms or diverse crops could recover, but smaller growers risked losing everything if the grapes failed.

8.8.3 Counterfeit and Low-Quality Wine

As trade grew, dishonest merchants saw chances to profit by selling poor-quality or fake wines labeled as something else. City governments and merchant guilds tried to stop these practices with inspections. They might require official seals or stamps on wine barrels. Some city-states introduced laws requiring tavern owners to buy from approved suppliers only. These measures helped protect the reputation of famous wine regions, though the problem of fraud never entirely vanished.

8.9 Scientific Inquiry and Experimentation

8.9.1 Early Wine Science

Although the scientific revolution came more fully in later centuries, Renaissance curiosity sparked new ways of thinking. Some landowners tested different pruning methods or planting densities, comparing results in small plots. Others wrote down fermentation times and outcomes, hoping to find patterns that led to smoother or longer-lasting wine.

Apothecaries (people who sold medicines) also took interest in wine, blending it with herbs or spices to create medicinal tonics. They believed wine could help preserve the healing powers of certain herbs and might have disinfecting properties. Though based on limited scientific knowledge, these experiments showed a growing desire to understand wine's chemical and natural processes.

8.9.2 Inventions and Tools

Devices like the **printing press** (invented in the mid-15th century by Johannes Gutenberg) allowed the wider spread of written materials, including agricultural manuals. This meant that ideas about wine production could reach more readers than before. While still a small percentage of people were literate, enough landowners, merchants, and educated monks could read to spread best practices quickly.

In some well-funded estates, rudimentary instruments measured temperature or moisture levels, though these were quite imprecise by modern standards. Still, they represented a shift toward observing and recording data about vines rather than relying solely on tradition.

8.10 Conclusion: Wine Poised for a Global Era

8.10.1 Impact of the Renaissance on Wine

The Renaissance brought economic growth, urban expansion, and a new appreciation for learning. Wealthy families and courts demanded better-quality wines, leading vineyard owners to experiment and refine their methods. Trade networks expanded by land and sea, carrying European wines farther than ever before. Artistic depictions and scholarly writings preserved knowledge about grape growing and fermentation.

8.10.2 Stepping into the Age of Exploration

As the Renaissance flourished, Europe stood on the brink of vast maritime exploration. Sailors and conquerors would soon plant vines in newly encountered lands, introducing wine production to the Americas, parts of Africa, and Asia. Meanwhile, established vineyards in Europe continued to flourish, improved by the cross-cultural exchanges, scientific inquiry, and commercial demands of the era.

CHAPTER 9

Wine During the Age of Exploration

9.1 Introduction

The Age of Exploration, also called the Age of Discovery, spanned roughly from the early 15th century to the 17th century. During this time, European powers—including Portugal, Spain, England, France, and the Netherlands—sent explorers across the globe. They sailed around Africa to reach Asia, crossed the Atlantic to reach the Americas, and later ventured into the Pacific. These expeditions changed the world forever, shaping economies, cultures, and diets on multiple continents.

Wine also took part in this global story. European settlers and conquerors carried grapevines to new lands, introducing wine production to the Americas and parts of Africa. At the same time, improved sea routes allowed European wine to reach faraway markets, while new goods—like sugar, spices, and cocoa—found their way back to Europe. In this chapter, we will explore how the Age of Exploration affected the history of wine, from planting the first vineyards in the "New World" to adapting old European practices to new climates.

9.2 European Powers and Their Quest for New Routes

9.2.1 Motivations for Exploration

By the 15th century, European merchants desired direct trade with Asia for valuable items like spices, silk, and precious metals.

Traditional overland routes through the Middle East were expensive and controlled by various powers, including the Ottoman Empire. This led countries like Portugal and Spain to seek sea routes around Africa or across the Atlantic.

While wine was not the primary motivation for these voyages, it quickly became part of the cargo. Crews took barrels of wine aboard ships for drinking (since fresh water could spoil on long journeys). Traders also brought wine as gifts for local rulers they encountered, hoping to open trade relations. These early voyages laid the groundwork for future settlements.

9.2.2 Portuguese and Spanish Explorations

Portugal's Prince Henry the Navigator sponsored expeditions down the West African coast. By the late 15th century, Bartolomeu Dias reached the Cape of Good Hope, and Vasco da Gama sailed on to India. Spain, on the other hand, sponsored Christopher Columbus, who reached the Caribbean in 1492. Later explorers like Hernán Cortés and Francisco Pizarro conquered vast empires in the Americas.

In both Portuguese and Spanish territories, Catholic missionaries and settlers soon arrived. Wine for the Eucharist became a necessity, so vineyards were planted in suitable areas. At first, settlers imported wine from Europe, but long sea voyages were risky. Bottles or barrels might spoil in the tropical heat, and shipping costs were high. Growing vines locally was more practical.

9.2.3 Other European Nations

England, France, and the Netherlands joined the global race, exploring North America, Africa, and parts of Asia. Again, wine was included among their supplies, though these countries were slower to plant vineyards overseas. Still, as colonial ambitions grew, more settlers tried to replicate the European diet—including wine—in their new homes.

9.3 Wine Crosses the Atlantic: The Americas

9.3.1 Early Spanish Vineyards in the Caribbean

After Columbus's voyages, Spain claimed many Caribbean islands and established early colonies. Initially, the settlers brought small amounts of Spanish wine stored in barrels. But the tropical climate—hot, humid, and prone to hurricanes—was not very friendly to grapevines. Vineyards in the Caribbean never thrived on a large scale.

Settlers often relied on shipments of wine from Spain or on other locally made alcoholic drinks (like fermented sugarcane juice, which later became rum). Still, some missionaries tried planting experimental vines. Records hint that they faced high disease pressure, with mildew and rot ravaging grapes in the warm climate. This experience taught colonists that not every area could support European grape varieties.

9.3.2 Mexico and Central America

The Spanish had more luck establishing vineyards in parts of mainland North and Central America with milder or drier climates. Hernán Cortés landed in Mexico in 1519, conquering the Aztec Empire. Soon, missionaries and settlers wanted local wine. They found that high-altitude areas in central Mexico, such as near modern-day Puebla, offered cooler nights. Vines shipped from Spain were tested there.

Monasteries and missions played a big role in early vineyard planting. Priests needed sacramental wine, and local populations needed a stable supply of alcohol that did not depend on risky sea voyages. Over time, grape growing expanded in suitable valleys. This formed the foundation of an enduring Mexican wine culture, although it faced ups and downs under various laws and policies.

9.3.3 South America: Peru, Chile, and Argentina

Spain also colonized large parts of South America, including Peru, Chile, and Argentina. These regions eventually became major wine producers in the "New World." Early Spanish settlers discovered that certain areas—like the Pisco region in Peru, the Central Valley in Chile, and Mendoza in Argentina—had climates similar to Mediterranean parts of Europe. They were dry, sunny, and had access to mountain water for irrigation.

Peru: Spanish settlers introduced vines to coastal and highland areas, producing wine and a grape-based spirit known as pisco.
Chile: Vines flourished in the central valleys, with moderate rainfall and long growing seasons. Missionaries planted grapes near Santiago and other cities.
Argentina: The Andean foothills around Mendoza offered abundant sunshine and meltwater from the mountains. Monks and colonists brought vine cuttings here, starting a tradition that would grow over centuries.

In all these lands, the first vines were often Spanish varieties such as the **Listán Prieto** (also called País in Chile or Criolla in Argentina). This grape adapted well to local conditions and became the backbone of early colonial wine.

9.3.4 North America: The Early Spanish Missions

Spain also ventured into what is now the southwestern United States, founding missions in Texas, New Mexico, and California. Franciscan priests, led by people like Junípero Serra in the 18th century, established a chain of missions along the Californian coast. They planted a grape known as the **Mission grape** (descended from the Spanish Listán Prieto).

These mission vineyards aimed to produce sacramental wine, but surplus often went to local settlers or trade. Over time, certain areas of California were recognized as having excellent soil and climate for grape growing. While true large-scale wine production in California would bloom much later (outside our current historical scope), the seeds were planted during this Age of Exploration.

9.4 Wine Goes to Africa and Asia

9.4.1 Portuguese on the African Coast

Portugal established trading posts along the western and eastern coasts of Africa, from modern-day Senegal down to Angola and around to Mozambique. Their primary interest was gold, ivory, and eventually slaves. While the climate in many coastal parts of Africa was tropical, some missionaries and settlers tried to plant grapes with limited success.

In Angola and Mozambique, for instance, the hot and humid environment made it hard for European grape varieties to thrive. Still, small pockets at higher elevations might have supported modest vineyards. Overall, African wine production remained small, mostly overshadowed by local fermented drinks or by imported wine from Europe.

9.4.2 The Cape of Good Hope

A significant exception was at the **Cape of Good Hope** (present-day South Africa). The Dutch East India Company established a resupply station at the Cape in 1652. Though the Dutch were not big wine producers themselves, they later welcomed French Huguenot refugees (in the late 17th century) who brought vine-growing expertise. This era is a bit later than the earliest Age of Exploration, but it shows how the seeds of wine culture spread.

Even before the Huguenots, some officials at the Cape grew grapes to provide fresh produce and wine for sailors on the long voyage from Europe to Asia. The mild Mediterranean-like climate around the Cape suited vines better than tropical regions. This laid the foundation for what would become a notable wine-producing region, although that fully developed in the centuries ahead.

9.4.3 Trading with India and East Asia

Portuguese merchants reached India in 1498, setting up bases in Goa and other coastal regions. There, they introduced European customs, including wine drinking. However, the Indian climate was mostly hot and humid, favoring local beverages over grape wine. Small vineyards might have existed in cooler highland areas or near coastal enclaves, but they did not become large-scale operations at this time.

In East Asia, particularly China and Japan, European wine arrived with merchants and missionaries, but it did not gain widespread popularity. Japan had a strict policy limiting foreign influence after the mid-17th century, so wine remained a niche curiosity. In China, rice-based drinks like **baijiu** and millet-based **huangjiu** had a strong tradition, leaving little room for imported grape wine. Nonetheless, small amounts of wine occasionally appeared at trading posts.

9.5 Sea Voyages and Wine Preservation

9.5.1 The Challenge of Long Voyages

Long-distance sea travel was difficult, with voyages to the Americas or around Africa sometimes taking months. Wine could spoil if exposed to heat, sunlight, or if the barrels were contaminated. Sailors sometimes drank cheaper wines, spiked with brandy to help it last longer. This practice of fortifying wine began as a practical solution, leading to styles such as **port** and **sherry** in later eras (though those fully formed a bit after our current timeframe).

Ships also faced storms, piracy, and the danger of rotting food supplies. Wine, if kept in sealed barrels and stored in cool parts of the ship, might survive better than fresh water. Still, many barrels arrived in the New World soured or partially evaporated. The risk and cost of shipping wine motivated colonists to grow their own vines whenever possible.

9.5.2 Barrels and Bottles

By the 16th century, coopers had refined barrel-making. Oak barrels became standard for transporting wine, as they were durable and could be rolled on and off ships. Glass bottles were still hand-blown, expensive, and not uniform in size. They were used more for serving wine at wealthy tables than for large-scale transport.

In some areas, explorers discovered native oak or other woods. They tried local timber for barrels, but not all woods were suitable—some added unpleasant flavors or leaked. Over time, European oak remained the preferred material for both storage and potential aging of wine.

9.5.3 Early Attempts at Fortified Wines

Though the formal creation of port, sherry, and Madeira wines would come into better definition later, the Age of Exploration planted the early seeds. Winemakers along trade routes learned that adding distilled spirits (like brandy) to wine helped it survive heat and motion at sea.

- **Portugal**: Ports near the Douro Valley eventually became known for "port wine," but that tradition would grow stronger in the 17th and 18th centuries.
- **Spain**: Areas like Jerez in southern Spain experimented with fortifying white wines, leading to styles that would be called **sherry**.
- **Portuguese islands in the Atlantic** (like Madeira) developed wines that also saw the benefit of fortification and heating, though the exact process would evolve over time.

Thus, the Age of Exploration spurred experimentation, shaping new wine styles that could handle ocean journeys.

9.6 Cultural Exchange and Wine Traditions

9.6.1 Native Populations and Local Drinks

In many places Europeans landed, they found indigenous peoples with their own traditions of fermentation—like chicha in parts of South America, pulque in Mexico, or palm wine in Africa. Over time, Spanish or Portuguese settlers sometimes mixed these local practices with European wine culture, creating unique hybrids.

Local inhabitants might have tried European grape wine out of curiosity or for trade. Some indigenous communities resisted adopting it, while others incorporated it into ceremonies or social events. This varied widely depending on local traditions, climate, and the type of interaction (peaceful trade or forced conquest).

9.6.2 Missionary Influence

Catholic missions had a powerful impact on shaping early New World wine culture. Priests needed sacramental wine, but they also introduced vineyards as part of teaching agriculture to local converts. Sometimes, missions offered small sips of wine during church services to local people. Over years, entire communities might learn basic grape-growing techniques, especially in areas with favorable climates.

9.6.3 Colonist Communities

European colonists, especially in places like Peru, Chile, and Mexico, continued to see wine as a link to their home cultures. They organized harvest festivals similar to those in Spain. Over time, a local identity began to form around the grapes and wine produced in the New World. Even though these wines might not have matched the complexity of Europe's best vintages at first, they offered familiarity to settlers thousands of miles from home.

9.7 Economic and Political Factors

9.7.1 Colonial Policies

European crowns often tried to control colonial production of wine and brandy to protect their domestic producers. For instance, the Spanish crown imposed laws to limit or tax wine production in the colonies, fearing competition with Spanish wineries. However, these rules were not always enforced strictly. Local settlers found ways to produce wine for personal use or local sale.

In some cases, colonial authorities demanded a portion of wine output as taxes or tithe. This practice mirrored Europe's feudal or royal taxes but adapted to colonial systems. Mission vineyards sometimes faced fewer restrictions if they could claim religious exemptions.

9.7.2 Trade Monopolies

Certain ports in Europe held official monopolies on trade routes. For example, the Spanish monarchy tried to centralize shipments of goods—wine included—through specific ports like Seville (later Cádiz). Portuguese shipments often had to go through Lisbon. This monopoly system aimed to keep taxes high and profits under royal control. Still, smugglers found ways to bypass these controls, selling wine or other goods illicitly.

9.7.3 Economic Impact in Colonies

Producing wine in colonies created new jobs and a new economic sector. Vineyards needed farmers, barrel makers, laborers, and transport services. As colonial populations grew, local demand for wine rose. Some colonists grew wealthy by supplying large estates, mines, or towns with wine. Meanwhile, indigenous workers often labored in harsh conditions on colonial farms, sometimes forced into labor systems that mirrored European feudalism.

9.8 Shipboard Life and Wine

9.8.1 Rations for Sailors

During the Age of Exploration, sailors on long voyages often had a daily ration of some form of alcohol—beer, ale, or wine, depending on the ship's origin. On Spanish galleons, wine might be part of the provisions if the route allowed for resupply from Spanish colonies. Because fresh water could spoil or grow algae, wine was considered a safer alternative, albeit one that could lead to discipline problems if sailors drank too much.

9.8.2 Celebrations at Sea

When ships crossed certain milestones—like the Equator or the Cape of Good Hope—crews sometimes held ceremonies or small celebrations. Wine (or other spirits) played a role in these events. Officers might share a better-quality wine with sailors to mark the occasion. These traditions contributed to sailors' morale on long, dangerous journeys.

9.8.3 Cultural Mixing Among Crews

Ship crews were often multinational. You might find Spaniards, Portuguese, Italians, Flemish, or even indigenous or African sailors forced or hired aboard. These diverse backgrounds led to shared meals and drinks. Sailors exchanged stories and tastes from their homelands. Wine, especially if it came from a crew member's region, became a point of pride or a reminder of home in far-off seas.

9.9 Legacy of the Age of Exploration on Wine

9.9.1 Global Spread of Grape Varieties

One of the most lasting effects of the Age of Exploration was the spread of Old World grape varieties to the Americas, parts of Africa, and eventually other places. While many of these early plantings were small and aimed at local needs, they laid the foundation for future wine industries. Over centuries, local farmers would adapt these vines to new soils and climates, creating unique regional styles.

9.9.2 Emerging Hybrid Cultures

In some regions, European grapes intermingled with native vines, though the success of these hybrids varied. Native American grapes existed in eastern North America, but they often produced what Europeans considered "foxy" or strange flavors. Early attempts to make wine from them were not very popular among European settlers. Even so, experiments with cross-breeding might have happened in scattered locations, setting the stage for a more robust hybridization process in later times.

9.9.3 Building Blocks for Future Waves

Though many of these colonial vineyards remained small or faced limitations from Europe's monarchy regulations, the Age of Exploration set the stage for the more extensive expansions of wine production that would come after. When political situations changed in the 18th and 19th centuries, some former colonies gained more freedom to cultivate their own wine industries.

CHAPTER 10

Wine in the 17th Century

10.1 Introduction

The 17th century (1601–1700) was a period of political upheaval, scientific awakening, and continued colonial expansion. In Europe, nations wrestled for dominance—leading to wars such as the Thirty Years' War (1618–1648). At the same time, thinkers like Galileo, Descartes, and Newton (toward the very end of the century) expanded human understanding of nature.

For wine, the 17th century represented a pivotal era. New trading patterns emerged as maritime powers grew stronger. Techniques in wine aging, storage, and even early bottling began to take shape. England became a significant force in shaping wine styles, thanks to its trade with Spain, Portugal, and France. In some areas, rising middle classes demanded better wine, pushing vineyards to innovate. This chapter will explore these shifts and how they laid the groundwork for future growth in the wine world.

10.2 Political and Religious Turmoil in Europe

10.2.1 The Thirty Years' War and Its Effects

The Thirty Years' War was a massive conflict in Central Europe, primarily affecting the Holy Roman Empire's lands (modern-day Germany, Czech Republic, Austria, and surrounding regions). It began as a religious dispute between Catholic and Protestant states but grew into a broader struggle involving France, Sweden, Spain, and other powers. Armies roamed the countryside, destroying crops and vineyards. Many villages were burned or abandoned, causing a sharp decline in wine production in some regions.

Once the war ended in 1648, rebuilding took time. Some vineyards were left untended for years, requiring replanting. Population losses meant fewer workers, leading to higher wages. Yet, the war also created opportunities for merchants who could supply wine to armies or to recovering towns. Over time, German regions like the Rhine and Mosel valleys bounced back, but scars remained well into the next century.

10.2.2 Shifts in Power: France, England, and the Netherlands

Outside Central Europe, France under Louis XIII and Louis XIV became a dominant force. French wines gained higher reputations in some markets, especially as aristocrats and wealthier townspeople demanded them. England, under the Stuart monarchs and then later under Cromwell's Commonwealth, continued to import wine from France and other places, even with occasional trade disruptions. The Netherlands emerged as a powerful maritime and commercial center, shipping goods, including wine, across the globe.

Despite occasional political tension—such as wars between England and France or Spain—wine trade managed to persist. Merchants found ways around blockades or used neutral ports to keep wine flowing to paying customers. In turn, this fueled the growth of wine regions in France and Spain that specialized in exporting to northern markets.

10.2.3 Colonial Rivalries and Wine

In the colonies, rivalries among European powers shaped who controlled key territories. The 17th century saw the Dutch controlling parts of Brazil briefly, the English seizing islands in the Caribbean, and the French establishing colonies in North America. These changes could disrupt or encourage local wine production, depending on the policies of the new rulers.

For instance, in the southwestern United States (still Spanish territory), Franciscan missions continued vineyard planting. In South America, Spanish authorities sometimes restricted large-scale wine production to defend the markets of Spanish producers. Yet local demand for wine was strong, so illegal or semi-legal wineries persisted.

10.3 Advances in Wine Storage and Bottling

10.3.1 The Emergence of Glass Bottles

Although glass bottles existed before the 17th century, they were costly and produced by hand. In the mid-17th century, English glassmakers, such as Sir Kenelm Digby, helped develop stronger glass by using coal-fired furnaces. This allowed for thicker, darker bottles that could withstand the pressure of aging wine.

Bottles became more uniform in shape, though there was still variety. Cork stoppers, cut from the bark of cork oak trees (found mainly in Portugal and parts of Spain), provided a tighter seal than earlier methods (like cloth or wax). This innovation meant wine could be stored longer without spoiling. Gradually, wealthier wine lovers began storing some wine in glass instead of in barrels. This shift laid the foundation for the practice of aging wine in bottles.

10.3.2 Corks and Corkscrews

Once bottles gained a standard design, cork stoppers became more important. Corks had been used in ancient times, but the 17th-century improvements in bottle-making made the use of cork more practical on a larger scale. A properly fitting cork kept oxygen out, preserving wine's freshness.

Corkscrews or "bottle screws" evolved to help remove these tight seals. Early designs appeared in the late 17th century, likely adapted from gunsmith's tools used for removing stuck bullets. These new tools made it easier to open a bottle without breaking the cork. Over time, the cork-and-bottle system became standard for finer wines, though barrels remained common for shipping large quantities.

10.3.3 Importance of Aging

With better storage in bottles and improved cellars, some wine connoisseurs noticed that certain wines tasted better after aging. Red wines from regions like Bordeaux and some robust reds from Spain could develop more complex flavors if left in the bottle. Though detailed scientific explanations for aging did not exist yet, experienced drinkers recognized the benefits of patience.

However, not all wine was meant for aging. Many everyday wines were still consumed soon after production, especially whites and lighter reds. Yet, the idea that wine could improve over time created a new market for "vintage" wines. Wealthy collectors started keeping track of good harvest years, storing those wines in private cellars.

10.4 National Tastes and Preferences

10.4.1 France: Growing Prestige of Bordeaux and Burgundy

In the 17th century, France's wine regions gained stronger recognition. **Bordeaux**, located in southwestern France, exported large amounts of wine to England and the Netherlands. Dutch traders sometimes used heat-based methods to create brandewijn ("burnt wine"), an early form of brandy, from Bordeaux and Charentes area wines. Meanwhile, inland, **Burgundy** became famous for high-quality red and white wines. The French royal court valued these wines, helping boost their status.

Cardinal Richelieu (a key figure during Louis XIII's reign) encouraged trade policies that benefited French wine, although local politics could complicate such measures. Over time, the concept of certain vineyards (especially in Burgundy) producing superior wines started to form. Monasteries remained active but gradually sold some lands to private hands, transferring vine expertise to lay growers.

10.4.2 Spain and Portugal: Sherry and "Portuguese Wine"

In Spain, the southwestern region around Jerez de la Frontera was known for a fortified wine that would become **sherry** (though that exact name and style took shape more fully later). English merchants showed strong interest in these wines, shipping them back to England. Some cargoes were relabeled or blended, leading to various styles known collectively as sack or sherris sack in English texts of the period.

Portugal's Douro region also saw growth in wine production, but the exact style we call **port wine** was not yet fully defined. Still, Portuguese wines made their way to England and Northern Europe, often fortified to survive the voyage. Meanwhile, on the island of Madeira, off the African coast, local producers discovered that wine stored in hot ship holds developed unique flavors. These were early hints of the famous **Madeira wine**.

10.4.3 England: A Thirst for Imported Wines

England's climate was too cool for extensive grape growing, except in very small pockets, and local attempts mostly yielded minor results. As a result, the English aristocracy and middle class drank imported wines—particularly from France, Spain, and Portugal. Taverns in London sold claret (a term the English used for red Bordeaux) and sack (various white wines from Spain). The growth of English trade and naval power in the 17th century made these imports more common.

English drinkers started to distinguish between different wine qualities. Some wealthier connoisseurs kept cellars to store casks or bottles. London coffeehouses (despite focusing on coffee and tea) occasionally served wine or brandy. Discussions about wine's merits grew among educated groups, setting a stage for future wine writing and criticism.

10.5 Trade Routes and Colonial Markets

10.5.1 Dutch and English Domination at Sea

By the mid-17th century, the Dutch Republic and England were the leading maritime powers, overshadowing Spain and Portugal, whose influences had peaked earlier. Dutch traders controlled shipping lanes in the Baltic, along European coasts, and even to Asia. They transported French and German wines to northern markets, sometimes stopping in English ports.

The English, after the Restoration of the monarchy in 1660, built a stronger navy and took colonial possessions from the Dutch (like New Amsterdam, which became New York). These expansions offered new markets for European wine. However, shipping wine across the Atlantic remained expensive, and colonial authorities often levied high taxes on imported goods.

10.5.2 Wine in the American Colonies

During the 17th century, English colonies on the North American east coast—like Virginia, Maryland, and the Carolinas—tried to grow European grapes with little success. The local climate, diseases, and native pests hindered these vines. Colonists tested native American grapes but found their flavors unfamiliar. A few small successes arose, but a robust wine industry did not emerge in these colonies at that time.

Instead, colonists imported wine from Europe or from the Spanish and Portuguese territories in the Caribbean and South America.

Wealthier colonists could afford expensive European wines. Meanwhile, cheaper rum and locally produced cider or beer became staples. Thus, wine was often reserved for the elite or special occasions in the English colonies.

10.5.3 Continued Growth in Spanish America

In Spanish America, including Mexico, Peru, Chile, and Argentina, vineyards planted in the 16th century continued to supply local markets. By the 17th century, these regions had established distinct wine-producing zones. In Peru, the Pisco region thrived on grape-based spirits; Chile developed central valley vineyards; Argentina expanded around Mendoza. However, the Spanish crown still enforced taxes and limits to protect Spain's wine industry. Smuggling and local black markets existed, showing the demand was stronger than official policies allowed.

10.6 Scientific and Cultural Changes

10.6.1 Early Scientific Writings on Fermentation

The 17th century saw the beginnings of modern science. While Louis Pasteur's work on fermentation would not come until the 19th century, earlier scholars started to examine chemical processes. Robert Boyle, for instance, studied gases and pressure. Though he did not focus on wine specifically, these breakthroughs eventually helped people understand how yeast converts sugar into alcohol.

Some landowners or "gentlemen scientists" kept notebooks on their vineyards, writing down observations about harvest times, grape quality, and fermentation problems. This approach, though still basic, laid a platform for future enology (the science of wine).

10.6.2 New Philosophical Attitudes

With the rise of rationalism and the Enlightenment spirit beginning to stir (especially toward the late 17th century), educated people questioned old traditions. They tried to classify wines more systematically, comparing flavors and regions. Writers discussed how soil, climate, and grape type might influence taste, although the term "terroir" was not widely used yet. This reflection hinted at more formal wine appreciation in the centuries ahead.

10.6.3 Art and Literature

Wine remained a popular theme in 17th-century art. Dutch still-life paintings, for example, showed tables laden with fruits, oysters, and half-filled wine glasses—symbolizing wealth and the fleeting nature of pleasure. In France, courtly scenes depicted lavish banquets with wine at the center. Meanwhile, English playwrights like Shakespeare (who died in 1616, but whose plays remained popular) referenced sack and ale, demonstrating wine's presence in daily social life.

10.7 Social Customs and Etiquette

10.7.1 Growth of Wine Taverns and Coffeehouses

In many European cities, taverns continued to serve wine to a mix of customers—travelers, merchants, artisans, and sometimes lower-ranked nobles. A new institution also rose: the coffeehouse. Coffeehouses became popular in England and parts of Western Europe, where people gathered to drink coffee, read newspapers, and discuss ideas. Although wine was not always the main focus in these establishments, some also offered wine or brandy.

Coffeehouse culture influenced how people socialized. While taverns were often raucous, coffeehouses aimed to be more polite and intellectual. However, the average person still frequented local alehouses or wine taverns if they could afford it. Drinking customs varied by region, but moderate consumption was often encouraged, with drunkenness viewed as shameful by many social and religious leaders.

10.7.2 Courtly Banquets and Middle-Class Dining

Royal courts and noble houses across Europe continued the tradition of grand banquets. These events showcased power and hospitality. Hosts served multiple courses, pairing certain dishes with wines from different regions. Some nobles prided themselves on their knowledge of exotic wines, possibly from the eastern Mediterranean or the Canary Islands.

A growing middle class in cities like Paris, London, and Amsterdam aspired to copy aristocratic dining habits (on a smaller scale). This included having wine at dinner parties or special occasions. Over time, this wider consumer base pushed up demand, encouraging vineyards to produce more consistent quality.

10.7.3 Health Beliefs

Physicians of the 17th century still used the ancient theory of the "four humors" (blood, phlegm, yellow bile, black bile). They sometimes recommended wine for certain ailments, arguing it could warm the body or aid digestion. At the same time, moralists warned of wine's dangers if taken in excess. King James I of England wrote against drunkenness in some of his writings, reflecting concern about public disorder. Despite these warnings, wine's allure remained strong.

10.8 Regional Highlights of the 17th Century

10.8.1 Bordeaux's Evolution

Bordeaux's wine trade with England and the Netherlands thrived, even with occasional interruptions. Dutch merchants sometimes drained marshy lands around the city, creating more vineyard space. Over time, certain areas like the Médoc were transformed into prime vineyard zones, though a full classification system would come later. Wine from Bordeaux, often called **claret** in England, developed a reputation for being elegant yet firm, especially as barrel and bottling techniques improved.

10.8.2 Burgundy's Refinement

Burgundy's monastic legacy passed into secular hands in many places, leading to noble or wealthy families controlling top vineyards. The idea that certain small plots (clos) produced superior wine continued to gain acceptance. Growers worked hard on pruning and soil care, aiming for the highest possible quality. The famous Pinot Noir grape thrived in these Burgundian soils, although it was not systematically identified as the region's chief red variety until later.

10.8.3 Champagne's Beginnings

Northern French vineyards around Reims and Épernay, known as Champagne, produced light, acidic wines. In the 17th century, some of these wines experienced a second fermentation in the bottle—often by accident—leading to bubbles. Although the creation of sparkling Champagne is often credited to Dom Pérignon (a Benedictine monk) in the late 17th century, the process was not fully understood at the time. Still, these early "effervescent" wines intrigued drinkers, setting the stage for Champagne's future fame.

10.8.4 The Rhine and Mosel

German-speaking lands tried to recover from the Thirty Years' War. Vineyards along the Rhine and Mosel saw renewed planting. The Riesling grape gained ground, although it was not yet the only variety. Some local rulers, like the Prince-Bishops of Würzburg, sponsored improvements in viticulture. Exporting these light, aromatic wines northward to the Baltic or westward to the Low Countries required stable trade routes, which gradually returned after the war.

10.8.5 Iberian Fortified Wines

In Spain's Jerez region and Portugal's Porto area, experiments with fortification and aging advanced, although the fully recognizable styles of sherry and port took clearer shape in the 18th century. Still, English and Dutch traders recognized these wines' durability at sea. Exported under various names, they earned favor in cooler northern climates.

10.9 Looking Toward Modern Changes

10.9.1 The Scientific Revolution and Enlightenment

By 1700, Europe was on the brink of the Enlightenment, a movement that would question old beliefs and emphasize reason. Science would slowly clarify the fermentation process, diseases affecting vines, and methods to preserve wine. Better glassmaking, improved transportation, and rising literacy all would shape the future of wine production and distribution.

10.9.2 The Rise of Nation-States

Over the next century, centralized nation-states like France and Britain would tighten control over trade, set tariffs, and engage in commercial competition. Wine taxes and regulations would influence which regions could flourish. Diplomatic relationships also mattered—when France and England were friendly, French wines poured into London taverns. When they were at war, imports fell, paving the way for alternative sources like Portugal's Douro region.

10.9.3 Colonial Expansion Continues

In the Americas, as colonies grew, more settlers arrived from Europe. They brought vine cuttings, knowledge, and tastes for familiar wines. Some colonists started new vineyards wherever the climate was suitable, although local obstacles persisted. Missionary expansions in places like California gradually formed a backbone for future industries.

10.10 Conclusion and Chapter Summary

10.10.1 The 17th Century's Mark on Wine

The 17th century was a bridge between the Age of Exploration and the modern era. Wars and political upheavals shaped who could grow and sell wine, while maritime powers transported it across seas. Glass bottling technology and cork stoppers began to transform wine storage, giving rise to the practice of aging certain wines.

10.10.2 Planting Seeds for the Future

New scientific curiosity hinted at better understanding of fermentation. Wine styles like Bordeaux reds, sherris sack (sherry), and early forms of Champagne were developing distinctive identities. Colonies across the globe continued small-scale vineyard experiments. Though many faced challenges, they kept European wine traditions alive in distant lands.

CHAPTER 11

Wine in the 18th Century

11.1 Introduction

The 18th century (1701–1800) was a time of great change in Europe and its overseas territories. The Enlightenment flourished, bringing new ideas about science, society, and government. Major wars and shifting alliances shaped trade routes and political borders. In many places, a growing middle class enjoyed increased wealth and sought better-quality food and drink, including fine wines.

These developments had a big impact on the wine world. Enlightenment thinking encouraged more systematic vineyard experiments, while new treaties and commercial agreements opened or closed markets for different wine regions. England, France, Spain, and Portugal—among others—competed for power on land and sea, influencing which wines were most available and fashionable. Meanwhile, colonial territories around the globe continued to adapt European grape-growing traditions to local conditions.

In this chapter, we will see how the 18th century's intellectual curiosity, political changes, and emerging consumer tastes shaped the production, trade, and culture of wine. By the century's end, many of today's famous wine regions had taken on clearer identities, setting the stage for further growth and challenges in the 19th century.

11.2 Political and Economic Background

11.2.1 Wars, Alliances, and Peace Treaties

The 18th century saw major conflicts like the War of Spanish Succession (1701–1714), the War of Austrian Succession (1740–1748), the Seven Years' War (1756–1763), and other regional struggles. These wars changed who controlled key territories and affected trade. When ports were blockaded or overrun, wine shipments might be halted or rerouted. Conversely, peace treaties could open new markets.

One notable agreement was the **Methuen Treaty** (1703) between Portugal and England, which gave preference to Portuguese wines in England if Portugal imported English textiles. This contributed to the rise of Portuguese wine sales in Britain, especially the fortified wine we now call **Port** (though it was still evolving in style at that time).

11.2.2 Rise of National Economies

As nation-states like Great Britain (united under the Acts of Union in 1707), France, Spain, and Austria-Hungary solidified, they created internal policies affecting wine. Taxes on imported wine became a key tool. For example, high duties on French wine in Britain led many British drinkers to choose Portuguese or Spanish alternatives.

In France, the royal government sometimes tried to control wine prices or supply, especially in Paris, to keep the populace happy. Elsewhere, local authorities might set tolls on wine crossing certain bridges or passing city gates. These taxes often made wine more expensive for consumers or more lucrative for traders, depending on the region.

11.2.3 Expanding Middle Classes

The 18th century also saw a growing middle class—merchants, skilled artisans, and professionals who had disposable income. These people desired "respectable" beverages to serve at social gatherings, leading to a rise in demand for wines from Bordeaux, Burgundy, the Rhine, Jerez, and Porto. Fine wine was no longer just for the royal court or high nobility. This shift stimulated vineyards to produce more consistent quality, brand their wines more clearly, and cater to evolving tastes.

11.3 Enlightenment Ideas and Wine

11.3.1 Scientific Curiosity and Viticulture

The Enlightenment encouraged observation, experimentation, and reason. Some landowners and scholars began studying grape growing in a more systematic way. They recorded data on soil, weather, and vine health. Though the exact science of yeast fermentation was still not fully understood, basic progress was made.

Writers and "gentleman farmers" published books about agriculture, sometimes including chapters on winemaking. They exchanged letters with fellow enthusiasts across borders, sharing tips on pruning methods or controlling vine diseases. This spread of knowledge, while modest compared to modern research, helped winegrowers adapt to climate shifts or new pest challenges.

11.3.2 Cultural Salons and Societies

In the 18th century, intellectuals gathered in salons, coffeehouses, and societies to debate philosophy, politics, and science. Wine often featured in these discussions. Some gatherings even hosted tastings or comparisons of different regional wines. A well-stocked cellar became a sign of refined taste. Poets and essayists praised wine's ability to inspire conversation and camaraderie, while also cautioning against excess.

The notion that wine could reflect the land it came from—like soils in Burgundy or the Douro—began to form a deeper impression on educated wine drinkers. Though the word "terroir" was still not standard outside French-speaking areas, the concept that a vineyard's location and conditions mattered was gaining acceptance.

11.3.3 Changing Views on Health

Some Enlightenment thinkers argued that moderate wine drinking was beneficial, providing nutrients and aiding digestion. Others warned against drunkenness and its social costs. Doctors debated the best "medicinal wines," prescribing them for various ailments. These discussions contributed to a broader acceptance of wine as a staple beverage, while highlighting the importance of controlled consumption.

11.4 Advances in Winemaking and Storage

11.4.1 Refinements in Fortified Wines

In regions like Porto (Portugal) and Jerez (Spain), the practice of fortifying wine with spirits to stabilize it during transport became more refined. By the mid-18th century, British merchants in Porto were carefully managing when to add grape spirit to the fermenting must, creating a sweeter, stronger wine—**Port** as we know it. Shippers recognized that English consumers preferred sweeter, robust wines that traveled well.

Likewise, in Jerez, producers perfected **sherry** styles, though the full classification (fino, oloroso, etc.) evolved gradually. Fortified wines found a strong market in Britain, Northern Europe, and even the Americas, since they could survive long sea voyages without spoiling as quickly.

11.4.2 Growth of Bottle Use

The 17th century introduced stronger glass bottles, and the 18th century saw them become more common among wealthier wine lovers. Cork stoppers improved, and some wine merchants specialized in bottling. While barrels remained crucial for aging and shipping, an increasing number of customers requested wines in bottles for private cellars.

Wealthy collectors began storing prized Bordeaux, Burgundy, or Madeira in special racks, keeping track of vintages. Wine merchants (called négociants in France, for example) stored barrels in their own cellars, bottling wines to order. This separation of production (by vineyard owners) and distribution (by négociants) influenced how wine was marketed and sold.

11.4.3 Barrel Aging and Blending

Certain regions honed their craft of blending wines from different vineyards or years to achieve a consistent style. Port producers, for instance, often blended various batches to match the desired profile. In Bordeaux, blending grapes like Cabernet Sauvignon, Merlot, and others became a more deliberate practice, aiming for balance and complexity.

Barrel coopers also improved their methods, selecting specific oaks for desired flavor. French oak from forests like Limousin or Allier was prized for its subtle impact on taste. Some vineyards tried different levels of barrel toasting, though this practice was still in its early stages. Overall, the 18th century saw a more purposeful approach to shaping a wine's final character through aging and blending.

11.5 Notable European Wine Regions in the 18th Century

11.5.1 Bordeaux and the Influence of British Trade

Bordeaux's strong connection to Britain continued despite periods of conflict. British merchants based in the city formed close ties with local châteaux, helping refine wines for the British palate. The wines were shipped down the Garonne River to the port of Bordeaux, then onto sea vessels bound for London, Bristol, and other English ports.

Wealthy English families often developed a taste for Bordeaux reds—called **claret**—leading to stable demand. Prices for the most esteemed estates rose, hinting at an informal ranking system. Though the official Bordeaux classification of 1855 was still decades away, the seeds of "first growth" reputations had already begun.

11.5.2 Burgundy and Its Monastic Legacy

Though many monastic lands were taken over by private owners, Burgundy retained its centuries-old vineyard parcels. Some of these clos (walled vineyards) had earned fame for producing exceptional Pinot Noir or Chardonnay. Wine from places like Beaune, Pommard, or Montrachet was prized at royal courts. Middle-class buyers also showed interest, though top Burgundies remained expensive.

Winemakers in Burgundy refined their methods, focusing on careful grape selection and gentle pressing. They recognized that poor handling could ruin Pinot Noir's delicate flavors. The concept of certain villages or climats (unique vineyard plots) having special qualities gained traction among connoisseurs, paving the way for later appellation systems.

11.5.3 Champagne: Early Sparkling Developments

In Champagne, accidental or intentional second fermentations in the bottle created sparkling wine. Houses like Ruinart (founded 1729) and

Moët (founded 1743) began commercializing fizzy Champagnes. Dom Pérignon, a Benedictine monk who died in 1715, was once thought to have "invented" sparkling wine, though many of these stories are romanticized.

English interest in sparkling Champagne also grew. Stronger glass bottles—often from English coal-fired furnaces—were better able to handle the pressure of carbonation, preventing explosions. Champagne's popularity among aristocrats and wealthy merchants made it a symbol of celebration and luxury, although the wine was still inconsistent in its sparkle.

11.5.4 The Rhine and Mosel in Germany

Germany's Rhine and Mosel regions continued to rebuild after the devastation of the Thirty Years' War. By the 18th century, Riesling had gained favor among some local estates. Noble families and church institutions reestablished vineyards along these rivers, producing lighter, aromatic wines. Exports to neighboring countries remained limited due to various taxes and conflicts, but German wines gradually reclaimed a place in the European market.

11.5.5 Iberian Peninsula: Port, Sherry, and Others

Portugal saw major growth in Port wine exports thanks to British demand. British firms set up in Porto, forging close ties with local growers in the Douro Valley. Spain's Jerez region refined sherry production for export, while other Spanish areas—like Rioja—remained mostly local in focus. Spanish authorities taxed and regulated wine shipments, but certain traders found success in big cities like Madrid or exported small quantities through coastal ports.

11.6 Wine Culture Beyond Europe

11.6.1 North America's Thirteen Colonies

In Britain's American colonies (which became the United States after 1776), attempts to grow European vines often failed due to local grape diseases and pests like phylloxera. Settlers in places like Virginia tried repeatedly, but success was limited. As a result, colonists imported wines from Portugal, Spain, and France, if they could afford them.

Wealthy families in cities such as Philadelphia, Boston, and Charleston sipped Madeira—fortified wine from the Portuguese island—because it traveled well. British taxes and mercantilist policies sometimes made it expensive, leading to smuggling or colonial frustration. Even after independence, American Founding Fathers like Thomas Jefferson loved fine European wine, especially from Bordeaux, though the new nation's domestic wine production was still minimal.

11.6.2 Spanish and Portuguese Colonies in Latin America

In Latin America, vineyards planted in the 16th and 17th centuries continued producing. Areas like Chile's Central Valley, Argentina's Mendoza, and Peru's coastal regions developed local wine cultures. However, Spanish laws often restricted large-scale wine exports to avoid competing with Spanish producers. Despite that, local demand in mining towns and cities fueled a steady internal market.

The trade of brandy or grape-based spirits (like pisco in Peru) also grew. Missionaries in Mexico and what is now the southwestern United States kept planting vines for sacramental wine, but large-scale commercial success was limited by official Spanish policies and the region's relatively sparse population.

11.6.3 The Cape Colony in Southern Africa

By the 18th century, the Dutch Cape Colony (in present-day South Africa) had seen the arrival of French Huguenots who brought vine-growing expertise. Estates in areas like Stellenbosch and Franschhoek developed, producing wine for local consumption and for passing ships. Some of this Cape wine found its way to Europe, where it was sometimes praised for its sweet and fortified styles (like the famed "Constantia" dessert wine). Though overshadowed by European wines, the Cape Colony's vineyards laid a foundation for future growth.

11.6.4 Asia's Limited Wine Adoption

Europeans in trading posts across Asia—like in India, China, or Southeast Asia—often imported their own wine. The climate in most regions was too tropical for successful viticulture with European grapes, though small experiments continued. Local populations had long-standing preferences for native drinks (beer-like beverages, rice wines, or distilled spirits). Thus, wine remained a niche product, mainly consumed by European settlers, traders, or local elites curious about foreign tastes.

11.7 Social Life and Celebrations

11.7.1 Growing Demand for Luxury and Pleasure

As the 18th century progressed, more people in Europe and the colonies had access to small luxuries. This included sugar, coffee, tea, and wine. Wealthy hosts showed off by serving imported wines or the latest fashionable types, like Champagne. Banquets, balls, and salons in cities like Paris, London, Madrid, and Vienna featured wine as an integral part of hospitality.

In France, **le Siècle des Lumières** (the Enlightenment era) was marked by refined dining, known as the art of the table. Cookbooks and etiquette manuals advised on how to serve wine, in which glasses, and in what order (usually white before red, lighter before heavier, though these rules were not fully standardized).

11.7.2 Mannerly Drinking and Temperance Calls

Along with the love for wine came growing concern over drunkenness. Clergy and social reformers worried about public disorder. In England, the **Gin Craze** of the early 18th century showed how cheap spirits could harm the urban poor. Wine, being more expensive, was associated with wealthier classes, but moralists still warned against overindulgence.

Some groups—small at first—advocated moderate or minimal drinking. They linked virtue with self-control. Yet, these voices did not dominate popular culture in the 18th century. Fine wine remained a hallmark of polite society, and social norms often praised a certain level of convivial drinking.

11.7.3 Music, Art, and Wine

Composers like Handel or Mozart wrote operas and chamber pieces often performed at gatherings where wine was served. Painters created scenes of feasts, still-life tables with fruit and wine, or pastoral vineyard vistas. Writers and poets praised wine's ability to spark conversation. This cultural emphasis helped shape an image of wine as both a refined beverage and a source of pleasure.

11.8 End of the Century: Revolutions and Shifts

11.8.1 The American Revolution (1775–1783)

The Thirteen Colonies' break from Britain caused disruptions in Atlantic trade. Some loyalists fled to Canada or returned to Britain, changing the demographics of wine consumers. However, American ports reopened to direct trade with France, fostering a relationship that would later allow American wine lovers, including Thomas Jefferson, to explore French wines more freely.

11.8.2 The French Revolution (1789–1799)

France was the center of European wine culture, so the revolution had a huge impact. Revolutionary governments confiscated church lands, including many vineyards, redistributing them or selling them to private buyers. This changed ownership patterns in regions like Burgundy. Nobles also lost estates, causing further changes. While chaos reigned in some areas, wine production did not vanish—it adapted to new social realities.

11.8.3 New Ideas about Property and Taxation

Revolutionary ideals in France and changes across Europe challenged old systems of privilege. Over time, these shifts affected how wine was taxed, traded, and consumed. More ordinary citizens gained the right to own land, including vineyards. Although the 19th century would see these changes unfold more fully, the seeds were planted in the 18th century's final decades.

CHAPTER 12

Colonial Wine Practices

12.1 Introduction

From the 16th to 18th centuries, Europeans carried their wine traditions to colonies across the Americas, Africa, and parts of Asia. They planted vines to ensure a local supply of sacramental and table wine, reduce import costs, and recreate a taste of home. Over time, colonial vineyards developed their own styles, influenced by native conditions and local labor forces.

In this chapter, we will look more closely at how wine was grown, made, and consumed in different colonies, focusing on the 16th through the 18th centuries. We will explore how colonial policies either restricted or encouraged local wine production, the impact of religious missions, and the adaptations settlers made to succeed in foreign lands. By the end, you will see how these colonial wine practices set the groundwork for eventual independent wine industries in places like South America and South Africa.

12.2 Spanish Colonies in the Americas

12.2.1 Early Mission Vineyards

Spain's empire in the Americas included vast territories in modern-day Mexico, Central America, and South America (especially the western regions). Catholic missionaries—Franciscans, Dominicans, and Jesuits—needed sacramental wine. Shipping wine from Spain was costly and risky, so they tried growing grapes locally.

They introduced European vine cuttings, usually from Spain's southern regions, including varieties like **Listán Prieto** (known locally as País or Criolla). Monasteries and mission stations became the first centers of wine production. These communities taught local indigenous or mixed populations how to tend vines, prune, and harvest. Over time, lay settlers also planted vineyards for personal or commercial use.

12.2.2 Laws and Restrictions

Spanish authorities worried that colonial wine might compete with Spain's own exports. At various times, they issued decrees limiting vineyard expansion or imposing taxes. This created tension between settlers who wanted to grow more grapes and officials who sought to protect Iberian producers.

In reality, local demand in mining towns, cities, and rural areas was strong. Many colonists continued or even expanded vine plantings illegally or by paying bribes. Smuggling networks allowed local wine to be sold where official regulations prohibited it.

12.2.3 Regional Developments: Peru, Chile, and Argentina

- **Peru**: Coastal valleys like Ica and Pisco became famous for grapes used in brandy-like spirits (pisco). Wine was also produced, though it often took a back seat to brandy.
- **Chile**: The Central Valley near Santiago offered Mediterranean-like weather, excellent for vines. Mission grapes thrived, and eventually some landowners experimented with higher-quality methods.
- **Argentina**: In the foothills of the Andes around Mendoza, irrigation from mountain snowmelt allowed vineyards to flourish. Jesuit missions played a major role early on, establishing the basis for what would become a significant wine region.

12.2.4 Social and Labor Structures

Colonial vineyards often relied on indigenous labor, coerced or contract-based, as well as the labor of people of mixed ancestry (mestizos). In some cases, enslaved Africans were also forced to work on estates. Large landowners controlled big haciendas or fincas, including vineyards. Smaller farmers might plant vines for extra income. The Catholic Church, through missions, also owned extensive land in certain areas.

12.3 Mexico and the North

12.3.1 Missions in Mexico

Starting in the 16th century, missions in central and northern Mexico planted vines for sacramental wine. Areas around modern-day Coahuila and Baja California eventually became notable for vineyard success. The hot, dry climate required irrigation, but certain high-altitude regions had cooler nights that helped grapes develop flavor without rotting.

Local authorities sometimes cracked down on large-scale winemaking, but missions often received special exemptions for religious purposes. They produced enough wine to serve local parishes and might sell or trade surplus to nearby settlers. Over time, even after Spanish control weakened, these mission vineyards stayed in operation.

12.3.2 The Northern Frontier: Texas, New Mexico, and California

In the northern frontier (present-day southwestern United States), Spanish missions were also crucial. As early as the late 17th century, missionaries in New Mexico grew grapes near the Rio Grande. Similarly, in Texas, small mission vineyards provided wine for Mass.

California saw the most lasting impact, especially in the 18th century when Father Junípero Serra founded a chain of missions along the coast. Each mission planted a vineyard of **Mission grapes** (descended from the Spanish Listán Prieto). While the volume remained small, these vineyards laid the groundwork for future development. After the missions were secularized in the 19th century, private ranch owners carried on or expanded winegrowing.

12.3.3 Interaction with Indigenous Peoples

In all these areas, missions used indigenous labor for vineyard tasks. Some natives adopted basic winemaking skills. However, native populations also suffered from diseases brought by Europeans and from cultural disruption. Wine became both a tool of religious practice and an economic resource for the missions. The complexity of this relationship—mixing forced labor, cultural exchange, and religious instruction—still influences local histories today.

12.4 Portuguese Colonies

12.4.1 Brazil

Portugal colonized Brazil in the 16th century, but the hot, humid coastal climate was not ideal for European grapes. Attempts at vineyards near coastal areas often failed due to disease. Settlers mainly relied on sugarcane to produce spirits (cachaça). However, in southern Brazil's cooler regions—like Rio Grande do Sul—some small-scale vineyard experiments occurred, though they did not fully thrive until later centuries.

12.4.2 African Outposts

Portugal controlled parts of coastal Africa, such as Angola and Mozambique. While these were mostly trading posts for slaves, ivory, and other goods, some settlers tried vines at higher elevations.

The scorching heat and tropical diseases often hindered success. As a result, wine in Portuguese African colonies remained a tiny niche. Most people there drank local fermented beverages or imported wine from Portugal.

12.5 The Dutch Cape Colony (South Africa)

12.5.1 Establishment and Early Vineyards

The Dutch East India Company founded a refreshment station at the Cape of Good Hope in 1652 to supply ships traveling between Europe and Asia. Early on, the settlers grew vegetables and raised livestock. Then, Jan van Riebeeck (the colony's first commander) planted vines, hoping to produce wine for sailors. By the 1680s, small but growing vineyards were supplying local demand.

12.5.2 Huguenot Influence

French Huguenots (Protestants fleeing religious persecution in France) arrived in the Cape Colony in the late 17th century. Some settled in areas like Franschhoek ("French Corner"), bringing knowledge of viticulture from regions like Burgundy or the Rhône. They improved planting techniques, pruning, and winemaking, helping the Cape produce better-quality wine.

12.5.3 Constantia and International Reputation

One of the most famous colonial wines was **Constantia**, a sweet dessert wine from vineyards near Cape Town. By the 18th century, Constantia had gained a reputation in European courts for its rich, sweet flavor. Kings and nobles in places like France, England, and Prussia prized it as a luxury item. While limited in quantity, it demonstrated that a colonial region could produce a wine that rivaled some European sweet wines.

12.5.4 Labor and Society

The Cape Colony relied on enslaved labor from Africa and parts of Asia to work the vineyards and farms. The social structure was divided between Dutch settlers, French Huguenots, a small number of free black or mixed communities, and a larger enslaved workforce. Despite the moral complexities, wine production grew steadily, supported by a stable local market (ships stopping at the Cape) and occasional exports.

12.6 French Attempts in North America

12.6.1 New France (Canada)

French explorers and settlers in parts of Canada (Quebec region) found that the climate was too cold for European grapes. Native grape varieties existed, but their flavors were unfamiliar to Europeans. Jesuit and Recollect missionaries made small attempts, though most wine had to be imported, often from France or via other colonies.

12.6.2 Louisiana and the Mississippi Valley

Further south, in French Louisiana, conditions were warmer, yet still humid. Settlers tried planting vines along the Mississippi, but success was limited. They often faced disease pressures, flooding, and a shortage of skilled vineyard labor. Imported wine from France or Spanish territories remained more common. Eventually, some hybrids between native grapes and European varieties would appear, but that lies beyond the 18th century scope.

12.7 Labor, Slavery, and Wine in Colonies

12.7.1 Forced Labor Systems

Many colonial wine estates, whether in Latin America or South Africa, used forced labor—either through enslavement or systems resembling serfdom. Enslaved individuals, indigenous workers under tribute, and indentured servants bore the brunt of vineyard toil. While these laborers learned agricultural skills, they rarely benefited financially. Wealth flowed to colonial elites or the Church.

12.7.2 Cultural Exchange

Despite the harshness of these systems, cultural exchange did occur. Workers brought new ideas, adapted tools, or introduced local pest-control methods. Over time, colonial wines sometimes blended European methods with local knowledge, creating distinct styles. For example, in Peru or Chile, the use of earthenware jars (tinajas) for fermentation or storage might reflect indigenous traditions mixing with Spanish practices.

12.7.3 Moral and Economic Debates

As the Enlightenment spread, some Europeans began questioning the morality of slavery. Others, especially colonial authorities and wealthy landowners, saw forced labor as essential for profits. The tension between economic gains and moral concerns simmered throughout the 18th century, though widespread abolitionist movements took stronger hold only in the 19th century. Still, these early debates hinted at the changes that would later transform colonial societies.

12.8 Trade Networks and Local Consumption

12.8.1 Local Markets

Colonial towns needed wine for religious services, social events, and daily consumption by certain classes. Tavern culture grew in port cities like Lima, Santiago, Buenos Aires, Havana, and Cape Town. Wealthier citizens sought higher-quality wine, sometimes imported from Europe if they could afford it. Middle and lower classes drank simpler local wines or other alcoholic beverages (like rum in the Caribbean).

12.8.2 Smuggling and Pirates

Strict mercantile policies forced many colonists to buy wine only from designated suppliers. This created opportunities for smugglers who illegally brought in barrels from rival powers or sold local wine in prohibited areas. Pirates and privateers also complicated matters, seizing cargoes of wine. Seafaring tales from the Caribbean or along the Spanish Main often involve stolen spirits and wine.

12.8.3 Changes in the Late 18th Century

By the second half of the 18th century, colonial markets were more robust. Cities grew, and some elites demanded the same fashionable wines popular in Europe—Champagne, Bordeaux, Port, etc. Meanwhile, local producers tried to improve quality. Though the crown or colonial governments still imposed restrictions, many colonists found ways to enjoy a variety of wines, shaping a more diverse wine culture in the colonies.

12.9 Impact of Revolutionary Movements

12.9.1 Shifts in Control

The late 18th century brought political unrest to many colonies. The American Revolution in the British colonies inspired other independence movements. In Spanish America, dissatisfaction with high taxes and limited trade freedoms grew. While significant revolutions in Latin America mostly occurred in the early 19th century, seeds of discontent were already present.

When colonial authority weakened, local winegrowers sometimes gained more freedom to expand. They no longer had to follow strict royal edicts or pay heavy taxes. However, wars for independence could also disrupt trade routes and damage vineyards. The transition periods saw uncertain times, but they also opened doors for new local initiatives.

12.9.2 Shifting Alliances

Colonial rulers changed hands in some regions—like the Dutch briefly controlling parts of Brazil earlier, or the French threatening Spanish possessions. Each new power brought new wine regulations or preferences. These shifting alliances sometimes favored certain wine styles (for instance, if the British took over a territory, it might become more open to imports of Port or Sherry).

By the century's end, the world map was in flux. Europe's own revolutions (in France, for example) further reshaped global connections. Colonial wine practices adapted to these changes, preparing to evolve further in the 19th century.

12.10 Colonial Wine Legacies and Chapter Summary

12.10.1 Foundations of Future Wine Regions

Even though many 18th-century colonial vineyards remained small or faced official limits, they set the foundation for future wine industries. Regions like Chile, Argentina, and South Africa would one day become global wine powers. Early missionaries, settlers, and local workers developed the initial skills and vine stocks that later generations refined.

12.10.2 Blending European Traditions with Local Realities

Colonists carried European grapes and methods across oceans. They had to adapt to different soils, climates, pests, and labor conditions. Sometimes they invented new techniques, mixing old-world knowledge with indigenous or slave-labor expertise. This process gave birth to unique styles and flavors not found in Europe alone.

12.10.3 Continuing Social Impacts

Colonial wine production was part of broader social systems, often based on inequality and forced labor. The profits from these wines enriched colonial elites and European powers. At the same time, it offered skills and possibly a modest livelihood for some local communities, though they rarely enjoyed equal benefits. As 19th-century independence movements spread, these vineyard traditions did not vanish—they often expanded under new leadership.

CHAPTER 13

Wine in the Early 19th Century

13.1 Introduction

The early 19th century (roughly 1800–1850) was a time of rapid political and social change around the world. In Europe, the aftermath of the French Revolution and the Napoleonic Wars reshaped nations and trade routes. In the Americas, new independent republics emerged after revolutions against Spanish or Portuguese rule, opening the way for shifting wine markets. Meanwhile, ongoing developments in science, technology, and social life continued to influence how wine was produced, sold, and consumed.

In this chapter, we will explore how wine adapted to the early 19th century's dynamic landscape. We will see how European nations adjusted vineyard ownership following the French Revolution, how the Napoleonic Wars disrupted trade in places like Bordeaux, and how newly independent regions of South America began to experiment more freely with their wine industries. We will also look at the ongoing evolution of wine culture, including changes in labeling, bottling, and the rise of new wine critics. By the end of this chapter, you should understand how the seeds planted in the 18th century began to sprout into more recognizable modern forms—still far from the fully modern era, but moving in that direction.

13.2 European Upheaval and Wine Trade

13.2.1 The Napoleonic Wars (1803–1815)

The Napoleonic Wars, involving Napoleon's French Empire against various coalitions (including Britain, Austria, Russia, and Prussia), disrupted European economies. Armies marched across vineyards, destroyed facilities, or requisitioned wine for troops. Coastal blockades and continental embargos crippled certain trade routes. For instance, Britain and France blocked each other's ports, hindering the flow of French wine to one of its largest foreign markets: Britain.

In Spanish and Portuguese territories, the Peninsular War (1807–1814) saw heavy fighting on the Iberian Peninsula. Vineyards in Portugal's Douro Valley and Spain's wine regions like La Rioja and Jerez faced interruptions to labor and commerce. Exports of Port and Sherry to Britain (and other places) continued in a stop-and-go manner, depending on local stability and shifting alliances.

13.2.2 Aftermath and Restoration

Once Napoleon was defeated and exiled (1814, then again in 1815), European powers convened at the Congress of Vienna (1814–1815) to redraw national boundaries. This ushered in a period called the "Restoration," where monarchies returned in places like France, Spain, and other regions. For wine, this meant a resumption of more stable trade, though tariffs and regulations remained complicated. Bordeaux slowly regained its British market, and port merchants in Portugal renewed ties with English importers.

Still, the early years of the Restoration were not entirely peaceful—uprisings and revolutions continued in various pockets (especially in the 1830s and 1840s). Yet, relative to the chaos of wartime, the 1815–1850 period gave vineyards time to recover and expand. European elites once again held lavish banquets, fueling demand for premium wines from places like Burgundy, Champagne, Bordeaux, the Rhine, Mosel, and Iberian fortified wine regions.

13.2.3 Shifts in Land Ownership

The French Revolution (1789–1799) had already confiscated church and noble lands in France, redistributing many vineyards to peasants or bourgeois buyers. By the early 19th century, some of these new owners were improving or expanding the vineyards. In Bordeaux's Médoc region, for example, drained marshland projects (started in the 18th century) were continued by investors who turned them into productive wine estates. In Burgundy, smaller plots emerged due to inheritance laws (the Napoleonic Code required equal division among heirs), leading to many fragmented vineyards, each carefully managed by different families.

Outside France, the Napoleonic Wars sometimes forced local land reforms, or monarchs reasserted control. The net effect was that wine production across Europe became more diverse in ownership, with new entrepreneurs entering the market. Some tried modern farming ideas, hoping to increase quality and profit.

13.3 Emergence of Independence in the Americas

13.3.1 Latin American Independence Movements

During the early 19th century, colonies in Spanish America fought for independence. Leaders like Simón Bolívar and José de San Martín played crucial roles in liberating regions that became Venezuela, Colombia, Ecuador, Peru, Chile, and Argentina. Meanwhile, Mexico also broke from Spanish rule in the 1820s, and Brazil separated from Portugal in 1822.

These transformations gradually loosened the restrictions that Spanish and Portuguese crowns had placed on local wine production. In the colonial era, Spanish authorities feared competition for Iberian wines, but as new republics formed, local growers could expand without as many legal barriers.

13.3.2 Chile and Argentina: Expanding Vineyards

Chile's Central Valley (around Santiago, the Maipo Valley, etc.) had mission vines from earlier centuries. With independence, landowners had the freedom to import new vine cuttings, experiment with improved techniques, and scale up production. Some aristocratic families, inspired by visits to Europe or by European advisors, attempted to refine local wines. By the mid-19th century, they started bringing in French varieties like Cabernet Sauvignon, setting the stage for Chile's future reputation (though the truly large-scale shift to French grapes came after 1850).

In Argentina, the provinces around Mendoza and San Juan enjoyed more autonomy. Skilled growers introduced irrigation infrastructure, enabling bigger vineyard expansions. Although local consumption of simple table wine remained dominant, the seeds for a more robust wine industry were planted. Over time, these developments would lead to Argentina's eventual global recognition for grapes like Malbec—though that, again, belongs more to the latter 19th century.

13.3.3 North America: The Early United States

The United States, after its independence (1776–1783) and the War of 1812 with Britain, gradually stabilized. Americans still mostly relied on imported wine, especially from Madeira, Port, Sherry, and occasionally French wines for those who could afford them. Attempts to grow European vines in eastern states continued to fail, thanks to native pests and diseases. However, some experimenters (like Nicholas Longworth in Ohio, though his heyday was in the 1820s–1840s) began planting local or hybrid grapes, paving the way for a modest wine scene.

In California, still under Spanish and then Mexican rule until 1848, mission vineyards persisted. The "Mission grape" (Listán Prieto) produced rustic wine for local consumption. True commercial expansion in California would wait until after it became part of the United States—beyond our immediate timeframe, though these early 19th-century missions laid the groundwork.

13.3.4 Brazil's Challenges

Brazil, having declared independence from Portugal in 1822, faced difficulties establishing vineyards in its hot and humid climate. Some German and Italian immigrants (arriving later in the 19th century) would eventually find success in southern Brazil's cooler hills, but during the early 19th century, the country's wine production remained very small. Sugarcane-based spirits and coffee exports dominated the economy far more than wine.

13.4 Advancements in Wine Production and Technology

13.4.1 Ongoing Improvements in Bottling

Following 18th-century innovations, glass bottles with cork stoppers became more widespread among wealthier wineries and merchants in the early 19th century. Bottle shapes varied by region—Bordeaux bottles had high shoulders, while Burgundies had sloping shoulders, and Champagne bottles were thicker to withstand pressure.

Bottling encouraged the concept of vintage wines, as it allowed wines from a specific year to be sealed and aged. Though not all consumers demanded vintage labeling, certain connoisseurs, especially in Britain and France, sought out "good year" bottles from their favorite regions. This slow shift toward bottling as a standard practice paved the way for more precise brand identity and recognition.

13.4.2 Cork Screw Innovations

The corkscrew continued to develop. Many were still handcrafted, with different designs appearing in Britain, France, and elsewhere.

Some had folding levers, others used helix shapes to remove corks easily. Wine enthusiasts of the time recognized the importance of a good corkscrew, as damaged corks could spoil a precious bottle.

13.4.3 Barrels, Coopers, and Aging

Barrels remained critical for both fermentation and transport. Coopers improved their craft, learning which forests produced oak with favorable flavors. French oak from Allier, Nevers, or Limousin, for example, was prized for subtle impact. Hungarian oak from the Tokaj region was also used in certain areas, especially around Central Europe.

Winemakers started to pay more attention to how long to age wine in wood. Over-aging could lead to oxidized flavors, while under-aging might mean harsh tannins. Some producers began to keep careful records of barrel times, blending older and younger wines to achieve balance. The early 19th century saw the seeds of "house styles," especially in fortified wines, but also in places like Bordeaux and Burgundy, where estate reputations were growing.

13.4.4 Emergent Tools and Machines

Though still pre-industrial in many ways, some regions experimented with basic mechanical aids. Hand-cranked grape crushers or presses with metal parts replaced all-wood designs in well-funded estates. These new presses could extract juice more efficiently. Scientists also used rudimentary thermometers and barometers to measure fermentation conditions, though a full scientific approach to winemaking was still in its infancy.

13.5 Shifting Tastes and Wine Criticism

13.5.1 Styles in Vogue

Tastes in wine varied by country and class. In Britain, sweet fortified wines like Port and Sherry remained popular among the upper and middle classes. Lighter clarets (Bordeaux reds) also maintained a steady following for those who could afford them. Champagne was increasingly fashionable among European aristocrats, though the cost of sparkling wine remained high, and production was still limited.

In France itself, the aristocracy and the new bourgeois classes enjoyed wines from Bordeaux, Burgundy, Champagne, and the Loire. Some wealthy Parisians took pride in hosting dinners with the best wines from each region, showing off their connoisseurship. Meanwhile, peasants and working classes drank local, inexpensive wines—often young, unaged, and served in simple taverns.

13.5.2 Emergence of Wine Writing

Early 19th-century newspapers and magazines sometimes included brief wine reviews or discussions of harvest reports. Intellectuals and travelers wrote diaries or letters describing wines they encountered. While not as formalized as modern wine journalism, these writings offered glimpses of quality assessments. Some merchants even began publishing short pamphlets to promote their wines, listing the advantages of certain vineyards or vintages.

Thomas Jefferson, though American, famously recorded his wine explorations during travels in France (late 18th century, continuing into the early 19th). His notes on Bordeaux and Burgundy influenced a handful of American elite. Although not widely published at the time, such personal accounts foreshadowed a future trend of wine criticism and collecting.

13.5.3 Role of Restaurants and Cafés

In France, after the Revolution, many aristocratic chefs opened restaurants serving refined dishes to paying customers. These establishments offered curated wine lists. Diners who once ate at noble mansions could now enjoy professional cooking (and associated wines) in a public venue. Over time, restaurants in Paris and other major cities set trends in pairing specific wines with courses, guiding middle and upper-class tastes. This phenomenon spread gradually to other capitals.

13.6 Cultural and Social Changes

13.6.1 Industrial Revolution's Influence

Though the Industrial Revolution primarily affected textiles, mining, and manufacturing, it indirectly impacted wine. Improved roads and the spread of railways (in the second quarter of the 19th century) made transporting wine barrels or bottles faster and less costly. Cities grew, leading to larger urban populations who demanded consistent supplies of wine. Over time, this would reshape distribution networks.

13.6.2 Temperance Movements

In parts of Europe and North America, small but vocal groups began advocating temperance or moderation in drinking. Religious societies, especially in Protestant regions, linked alcohol abuse to social problems. However, these movements mostly targeted hard liquors like gin or whiskey, viewing wine as somewhat less harmful—especially if consumed at meals. The full rise of powerful temperance movements would come later in the 19th century.

13.6.3 Wine in Political Symbolism

During the Napoleonic era, references to wine sometimes appeared in propaganda, depicting soldiers drinking celebratory toasts after victories. In newly independent Latin American nations, wine occasionally symbolized cultural pride or progress. In France, the phrase "Liberté, Égalité, Fraternité" might be toasted with local wine. These political connections show how wine was interwoven with evolving national identities.

13.7 Notable Regional Highlights

13.7.1 France: Bordeaux, Burgundy, Champagne

- **Bordeaux**: After the Napoleonic Wars, British demand for claret picked up. Some châteaux expanded cellars and refined techniques. Early critics praised wines from notable estates in the Médoc and Graves.
- **Burgundy**: Smaller vineyard ownerships due to Revolutionary laws led to many separate parcels. Still, certain vineyards upheld reputations. Winemakers strove to perfect Pinot Noir and Chardonnay, even if science was limited.
- **Champagne**: Production of sparkling wine increased slowly. Houses like Moët, Veuve Clicquot (established in 1772, but rising in prominence in the early 1800s), and others tested ways to control secondary fermentation. Champagne grew as a luxury item among European elites.

13.7.2 Iberian Peninsula: Port, Sherry, and More

- **Portugal**: The Port industry consolidated around British merchants in Porto and Vila Nova de Gaia. They refined fortification timing and aging in "lodges" near the Douro River's mouth. Some early brand names emerged, though formal brand identity was still developing.
- **Spain**: In Jerez, Sherry production expanded, with casas de viña (vine houses) focusing on traditional solera systems. Rioja remained mostly local in scope, yet some forward-thinking landowners began adopting French oak barriques (though this would truly accelerate later, in the mid-to-late 19th century).

13.7.3 Germany and Central Europe

The early 19th century saw the German Confederation form after Napoleon's defeat. Vineyards along the Rhine, Mosel, and Main Rivers stabilized, producing primarily Riesling and other white grapes. Noble or princely estates led the way in quality, with some experimenting in sweet late-harvest styles. The Austrian Empire likewise maintained traditional vineyard areas in Lower Austria, Styria, and parts of Hungary—Tokaj in Hungary being famed for sweet Tokaji Aszú. Political changes occasionally shuffled ownership, but the wine trade persisted mostly within central European markets.

13.7.4 South Africa: Cape Wines

Under British rule after 1806, the Cape Colony continued to produce wine. Constantia sweet wine remained a prized export in European courts. British policy sometimes favored Cape wine imports, especially when blocking French wines during the Napoleonic Wars. However, as peace returned, competition from European producers made it harder for Cape wines to maintain a high price. Yet, the colony's vineyards had grown enough for a steady local market.

13.8 Obstacles and Challenges

13.8.1 Vine Diseases (Before the Major Outbreaks)

Although the 19th century would later witness devastating vine diseases like powdery mildew (oidium) and phylloxera, these had not yet exploded in the early decades. Nevertheless, smaller-scale problems—mildew, rot, and occasional pest infestations—persisted. Growers handled them through sulfur dusting (known from the 18th century), orchard hygiene, and luck with the weather. The real crisis of phylloxera would strike in the mid-to-late 19th century, which we will address in Chapter 14.

13.8.2 Transportation and Preservation

Despite improvements, roads were often rough, and long-distance shipping of wine could lead to spoilage. Wines that traveled best were fortified or had strong tannins (like some Bordeaux). Shipping across oceans, as in the case of Madeira, Sherry, and Port, remained expensive. Breakage of glass bottles was common. While barrels were sturdy, they allowed gradual oxidation, affecting wine quality over time.

13.8.3 Limited Scientific Understanding

Though the Enlightenment boosted rational thought, the detailed biology of fermentation and vine diseases was not well understood. Winemakers relied heavily on tradition and trial-and-error. If a vintage was poor due to rain or frost, there was little recourse beyond basic vineyard management. While some landowners paid attention to chemistry, truly systematic enology would not gain momentum until the mid-19th century and beyond.

13.9 Transition to Mid-19th Century

13.9.1 Growing Knowledge Exchange

By the 1840s, more travelers, merchants, and diplomats crisscrossed Europe and the Americas. They swapped tips about vineyards, cellar techniques, and newly fashionable wine styles. Railroad construction (especially after 1830 in England, later in France and Germany) hinted at faster, cheaper trade—crucial for perishable wine.

13.9.2 Seeds of Future Classifications

The notion that certain estates or vineyard plots regularly produced finer wine was increasingly recognized. In Bordeaux, brokers categorized châteaux informally by reputation and price. In Burgundy, the concept of "cru" (a recognized, high-quality vineyard) existed historically but was mostly local knowledge. Over the coming decades, these ideas would crystallize into official classifications, eventually culminating in famous rating systems like the Bordeaux 1855 Classification.

CHAPTER 14

The Spread of Vine Diseases and Their Impact

14.1 Introduction

The 19th century brought not only political revolutions and industrial changes but also biological invasions that nearly destroyed Europe's (and much of the world's) vineyards. Chief among these threats was **phylloxera**—a tiny aphid-like insect that attacks vine roots. Before phylloxera arrived, earlier waves of diseases like **powdery mildew** (oidium) and **downy mildew** also challenged growers. Together, these outbreaks forced wine producers to adopt radical new methods, including chemical treatments and, eventually, grafting European vines onto resistant American rootstocks.

In this chapter, we will examine how these vine diseases emerged, spread, and affected different wine regions. We will see how phylloxera—initially unknown in Europe—was accidentally introduced and caused havoc from the 1860s onward. While this time period overlaps with the mid-to-late 19th century, the story of vine diseases is so crucial that it deserves its own dedicated chapter here. We will keep our main historical focus without venturing into late 20th-century developments, yet we must discuss enough detail to show how growers battled these threats and reshaped the wine world.

14.2 Early Disease Outbreaks Before Phylloxera

14.2.1 Powdery Mildew (Oidium)

Powdery mildew, or **oidium**, is a fungal disease that first appeared in European vineyards around the mid-19th century (1840s–1850s).

Believed to have come from North America, it spread quickly, covering vines with a white, powder-like coating that harmed leaves and grape bunches. Growers noticed reduced yields and lower-quality fruit. Some believed it was a sign of poor "air" or cosmic influences, as true fungus biology was still poorly understood.

The search for remedies led to the use of sulfur dusting. Sulfur, when applied correctly, helped control oidium's spread. By the time phylloxera emerged, many European vineyard owners had discovered that sulfur could be a potent ally against fungal infections. Still, sulfur had to be reapplied frequently and carefully, and not all areas could afford or implement it effectively.

14.2.2 Downy Mildew

Downy mildew, another fungal disease, arrived a bit later (historically noted around the 1870s) from the Americas. It would become a major scourge in many humid regions. Infected vines developed yellowish, oily patches on leaves, then white fuzz on the undersides of those leaves. This disease also severely reduced yields. Eventually, vineyard owners turned to copper-based sprays like the **Bordeaux mixture** (a blend of copper sulfate and lime) to control downy mildew. But in the initial encounters, many growers were unprepared.

14.2.3 Impact on Practices

Even before phylloxera, these fungal diseases forced vineyard owners to become more vigilant, adopting repeated spraying or dusting. It also spurred some interest in pest-resistant vine varieties, though Europeans typically dismissed local American vines due to their "foxy" aromas. As we will see, the ultimate crisis of phylloxera would change those opinions drastically.

14.3 Phylloxera: The Tiny Destroyer

14.3.1 Origin in North America

Phylloxera (**Daktulosphaira vitifoliae**) is an insect native to North American grape species. American vines coevolved with it, developing natural resistance. However, European **Vitis vinifera** had no such defenses. When phylloxera was accidentally introduced to Europe—most likely via imported American vine cuttings in the 1850s or early 1860s—it found a perfect host.

The insect lives part of its life cycle feeding on leaves, but the most devastating effect occurs when it attacks vine roots, creating galls and eventually killing the plant by blocking nutrient and water uptake. Because phylloxera multiplies quickly, it spreads from vineyard to vineyard, wiping out entire fields within a few years.

14.3.2 First Discoveries in France

Historically, the earliest recognized outbreak was near the Rhône region of France in the early 1860s (some accounts say 1863 near Languedoc). At first, growers were baffled: vines turned yellow, stunted, and died, but no obvious disease like fungus was to be seen on leaves or fruit. Scientists investigating the dead roots finally found tiny insects. By the time they realized phylloxera's threat, it had already spread widely.

Governments, especially in France, declared emergencies. Agricultural societies offered rewards for cures. Quarantine laws tried to restrict vine movement. But phylloxera often travels underground or clings to equipment, so containment proved nearly impossible. Within a few decades, the plague reached most major wine regions of Europe.

14.3.3 Panic and Economic Crisis

Phylloxera destroyed livelihoods. France, the world's largest wine producer, faced a severe wine shortage in the 1870s and 1880s. Some local economies collapsed, as entire vineyard areas had to be abandoned. Workers lost jobs, merchants lost stocks, and many families faced ruin. Wine prices soared, encouraging adulteration and fraud—some unscrupulous sellers mixed sugar, water, or foreign wines to stretch supplies.

Other countries in Europe eventually faced the same fate. Spain, Portugal, Italy, Germany, and even parts of the Austrian Empire and the Balkans discovered phylloxera in their vineyards over the ensuing decades. Where it arrived, devastation followed. Some remote regions with sandy soils, where phylloxera struggles to survive, escaped major damage, but they were exceptions.

14.4 Attempted Solutions

14.4.1 Chemical Treatments and Flooding

Early proposals ranged from flooding vineyards (since prolonged submersion could kill phylloxera) to injecting carbon bisulfide or other toxic chemicals into the soil. Flooding worked only in areas with abundant water and well-structured fields—mainly in certain flat regions. Chemical treatments were expensive and hazardous, and they offered only temporary relief.

14.4.2 Searching for a Miracle Cure

Scientific committees tested thousands of substances—mercury compounds, carbolic acid, or even exotic concoctions. None provided a safe, permanent fix. Growers who tried to continue with vinifera vines often faced repeated infestations. Meanwhile, cross-border tensions arose: governments blamed traveling merchants or tourists for spreading the pest, leading to fierce quarantines that stifled trade of vine cuttings.

14.4.3 Discovering Grafting

Eventually, some horticulturalists realized that American rootstocks (from species like **Vitis riparia**, **Vitis rupestris**, or **Vitis berlandieri**) resisted phylloxera. European vinifera scions—carrying desired grape variety traits—could be grafted onto these American roots, combining resistance with classic European flavor. At first, many French growers disliked American vines, claiming they produced off-flavors. But as phylloxera ravaged the land, they learned that only rootstock grafting could truly solve the problem.

By the late 19th century, grafting onto American rootstocks became the standard approach. This solution arrived too late for many small farmers who had already lost everything. But gradually, replanting with grafted vines restored Europe's vineyards, ensuring future generations could still drink wines made from traditional European varieties, albeit with American roots beneath.

14.5 Geographical Spread and Timeline

14.5.1 France, Spain, and Beyond

- **France**: Phylloxera started in the south, then moved to Bordeaux, Burgundy, Champagne, and the Loire by the 1880s. Each region lost the majority of its vines before adopting grafting.
- **Spain and Portugal**: Slightly later, the pest invaded Iberia. Spain's Rioja region ended up replanting with modern techniques, inadvertently ushering in the use of French oak. Portugal's Douro Valley also had to graft, though some mountainous sites with poor soils were spared.
- **Italy**: Different subregions encountered phylloxera at varying times. Tuscany, Piedmont, and Veneto eventually had to replant. The patchwork of soils and microclimates meant some pockets remained phylloxera-free for a while, but the pest eventually reached them.

14.5.2 Central Europe, the Balkans, and Germany

Germany, Austria-Hungary, and Southeastern Europe discovered phylloxera creeping in by the late 19th century. Again, some sandy riverbanks or cold zones escaped for a time, but most significant wine areas were attacked. The cost of replanting was huge, but large estates often managed better than smallholders.

14.5.3 Beyond Europe

Phylloxera also traveled internationally. South American vineyards began to see it in the late 19th or early 20th century, though Chile's geographical barriers (the Andes, deserts, and ocean) famously delayed its arrival. South Africa, Australia, and other New World regions encountered it too, forcing them eventually to adopt grafted rootstocks. However, each region had its own timeline and occasionally avoided the worst damage thanks to quarantine or natural barriers.

14.6 Consequences for Wine Quality and Diversity

14.6.1 Changes in Varieties

Some old European varieties vanished or declined if they were deemed not worth replanting. Meanwhile, popular French grapes—like Cabernet Sauvignon, Merlot, Syrah, Chardonnay, etc.—became more widespread because growers found it easier to replant with known "successful" varieties on American rootstock. This shift led to a certain standardization over time, though that effect fully emerged later.

14.6.2 Modernizing Vineyard Methods

Forced replanting often meant adopting better training systems, spacing, and disease-control measures. Many vineyards installed new trellises or used modern pruning advice from agricultural schools that emerged in the late 19th century. This modernization had a silver lining: yields and quality improved in some cases, ironically because phylloxera forced a restart.

14.6.3 Rise of Scientific Institutions

Phylloxera spurred governments and landowners to invest in agronomic research. Institutions like the **Montpellier school of agriculture** in France studied ampelography (grape identification), rootstock breeding, and pest control. Over time, scientists made breakthroughs in plant pathology, soil science, and genetics. Though these institutions would shape the 20th century significantly, their roots lie in this 19th-century crisis.

14.7 Social and Economic Impact

14.7.1 Rural Exodus and Bankruptcy

In Europe, many small winegrowers went bankrupt or emigrated when phylloxera destroyed their livelihoods. Some headed to cities to find industrial work. Others moved overseas to places like North or South America, sometimes bringing vine knowledge with them. This population shift changed the face of rural communities in places like France's Languedoc or Italy's Piedmont.

14.7.2 Wine Prices and Fraud

During the height of the phylloxera devastation, wine supply dropped drastically. Prices rose, leading to frequent adulteration. Unscrupulous merchants sold "wine" blended with sugar, water, and artificial coloring. Governments tried to crack down, passing early labeling or purity laws. This scenario revealed the need for stricter regulations, foreshadowing modern appellation systems and wine standards.

14.7.3 Grafting Workforce

Grafting enormous tracts of vineyards was labor-intensive. Skilled grafters—often traveling specialists—moved from region to region, splicing American rootstocks to European cuttings. This created a new niche job market. Some local workers learned these techniques, thereby gaining valuable skills. Over time, it became the norm to start a vineyard with grafted rootstock, forever changing the tradition of planting "own-rooted" vines in Europe.

14.8 Recovery and Long-Term Effects

14.8.1 Gradual Replanting

The replanting process took decades. Some regions started in the 1870s, others in the 1890s or even early 20th century. Where vine densities were high, owners replaced old vines incrementally. Progressive estates used the opportunity to reorganize parcels, introduce spacing for easier plowing or mechanical aids, and plant uniform rows. Over time, many European vineyards ended up with a more standardized layout than the patchwork preceding phylloxera.

14.8.2 Emergence of Cooperative Wineries

As small growers struggled to afford replanting, cooperative cellars began to form (especially in France, Italy, and parts of Spain). These cooperatives pooled resources, shared modern equipment, and purchased rootstocks collectively. This cooperative movement fostered a sense of solidarity in many rural communities, enabling them to survive the crisis and compete against large estates.

14.8.3 Influence on Global Winemaking

Once the solution—grafting—was established, it spread worldwide. Newly developing regions like California or Australia soon embraced rootstocks to protect against phylloxera. European knowledge of grafting also improved viticulture academically, leading to new fields of study. By the end of the 19th century, the wine world was irreversibly changed, with every major region adopting some form of protective measure against phylloxera and other pests.

14.9 Cultural and Scientific Reflections

14.9.1 Phylloxera in Literature and Art

The devastation of vineyards and the resulting social upheaval occasionally appeared in literature or political cartoons. Some French novels or poems lamented the dying vines. Illustrations showed heroic farmers battling insect plagues, reflecting the era's sense of crisis. While not as commonly depicted as, say, war or industrialization, phylloxera left a deep mark on the cultural consciousness in winegrowing regions.

14.9.2 Growth of Enological Science

Agricultural societies, research stations, and universities began focusing on vines and wine as legitimate subjects of study. Ampelography—the classification and identification of grape varieties—became essential to ensure correct pairing of scions and rootstocks. Chemistry labs analyzed soils, tested fungicides, and studied fermentation. Although these developments accelerated in the late 19th century, the impetus came largely from the phylloxera-driven crisis.

14.9.3 Legacy of Rootstock Use

To this day (in many historical contexts), nearly all European Vitis vinifera vines are grafted onto American or hybrid rootstocks. Even though some pockets of Europe (like parts of Chile's vineyards, certain sandy soils in Spain or the Canary Islands) still have ungrafted vines, the universal acceptance of grafting stands as a direct outcome of the 19th-century phylloxera invasion. It also opened the door to crossbreeding experiments that produced new, more resistant varieties.

CHAPTER 15

Wine in Cultural Ceremonies and Celebrations

15.1 Introduction

From ancient myths to religious rites and seasonal festivals, wine has held a central place in ceremonies around the world for thousands of years. It has symbolized fertility, harvest, sacrifice, and joy. People have used wine to honor gods and goddesses, seal treaties, celebrate weddings, and mourn the dead. By looking at these traditions, we learn how wine became more than just a drink—it became a cultural marker that brought communities together.

In this chapter, we will explore how ancient civilizations viewed wine in their rituals, how it found a permanent role in major world religions, and how it appeared in everyday celebrations such as marriages and feasts. We will travel through time, from the early evidence of wine in prehistoric communal gatherings to its role in major festivals of ancient Greece and Rome, to its place in Jewish and Christian ceremonies. Along the way, we will see how different societies shaped their practices around wine and how these customs evolved through centuries.

15.2 The Earliest Rituals and Communal Gatherings

15.2.1 Prehistoric Roots

Before written history, people likely discovered the effects of fermented grape juice by accident. Early hunter-gatherers might have gathered wild grapes, and once they realized the juice could ferment, they used it in communal gatherings or feasts. Archaeological evidence, like residues on pottery, suggests that by the Neolithic era, humans intentionally produced and consumed wine as part of community bonding.

In many prehistoric sites, experts have found large communal spaces or structures that may have been used for feasting. It is reasonable to assume that when wine was available, it took on a magical or special role—partly because of its intoxicating effects, and partly because fermentation was mysterious in those days. If someone felt relaxed, cheerful, or even lightheaded from drinking, it could be interpreted as a sign of divine presence or blessing.

15.2.2 Wine and Ancient Spiritual Beliefs

As humans formed stable farming communities, wine often emerged as a ritual drink tied to fertility or weather gods. In these early agrarian societies, a successful grape harvest required favorable climate conditions. Drinking wine became a way to celebrate the harvest, give thanks to deities for bounty, or even attempt to ensure future prosperity.

In some regions, burial sites have revealed vessels containing wine or traces of fermented beverages. The presence of wine in a tomb might mean it was intended to accompany the deceased into the afterlife, reflecting a belief that wine was precious and needed beyond earthly life. These traditions laid the groundwork for more elaborate ceremonies in the eras to come.

15.3 Ceremonial Wine in Ancient Civilizations

15.3.1 Ancient Egypt

Wine had a special role in Egyptian religion and afterlife beliefs. Tomb paintings show pharaohs and nobles enjoying wine, and jars of wine were placed in tombs to provide for the deceased. Certain deities, like Hathor (associated with joy and fertility), were linked to drunken revelry. One myth even describes how the goddess Sekhmet was subdued by a red-colored drink that appeared to be wine, saving humanity from her wrath.

During festivals, Egyptians offered wine to the gods in temples. Priests poured wine over altars or statue bases, believing that the gods would consume its essence. Royal banquets, often associated with religious or state celebrations, featured abundant wine as a mark of prestige. Though beer was more common among the general populace, wine took on a ceremonial status for the upper classes and in worship rites.

15.3.2 Mesopotamia

In Mesopotamia, wine carried prestige, often reserved for religious temples, royalty, and the wealthy. Ceremonies for gods like Ishtar or Marduk included offerings of food and drink. Feasting in temple courtyards might incorporate communal consumption of wine, symbolizing unity between worshippers and their deities.

Many texts and administrative records from Sumerian or Babylonian temples mention wine rations for priests or gifts for gods. Although beer dominated daily life, wine's cost and relative rarity elevated it in religious contexts. Sharing wine at festivals reaffirmed social ties and honored spiritual forces.

15.3.3 Ancient Greece: Dionysus and Symposia

In ancient Greece, the god **Dionysus** (Bacchus to the Romans) personified wine, fertility, and religious ecstasy. Festivals like the **Dionysia** were held in his honor, featuring processions, theater performances, and plenty of wine-drinking. Dionysus was believed to inspire creativity, madness, or joy—outcomes linked to the unpredictable effects of wine.

Symposia were structured drinking gatherings among Greek male citizens. While not strictly a religious ceremony, the symposium had strong cultural significance. Participants reclined on couches, drank wine diluted with water, and engaged in philosophical discussion, music, and poetry. Before drinking, they offered a libation—a small pour of wine on the ground—to the gods. This ritual recognized the divine presence in their gathering, blending social pleasure with a hint of sacred observance.

15.3.4 Roman Religion and Festivals

The Romans continued Greek traditions and identified their own gods, calling the wine deity **Bacchus**. The festival **Bacchanalia** was initially a secret, wild celebration that alarmed the Roman Senate, which attempted to ban or regulate it. Despite controversies, Bacchus and wine remained part of public and private worship.

Romans believed wine was essential for religious ceremonies, from household rituals (pouring a small offering for the **Lares** or **Penates**—household gods) to large-scale festivals at temples. During triumphs or official feasts, officials and priests poured wine as a libation. Roman banquets (convivia) often featured toasts to gods or ancestors, blending spiritual and social elements seamlessly.

15.4 Major Religious Traditions and Wine

15.4.1 Judaism

In Judaism, wine holds a prominent place in religious life. It is used in blessings (Kiddush) to sanctify the Sabbath (Shabbat) and festivals. During **Passover**, four cups of wine are consumed at the Seder meal, symbolizing redemption and freedom from slavery in Egypt. Wine also appears at weddings, circumcision ceremonies, and other life-cycle events.

Historically, wine production in Jewish communities had to follow certain dietary laws (kashrut). Wine could only be handled by those following Jewish law to retain its kosher status. In ancient times, this reinforced a sense of community and identity. Even when Jewish populations were spread across different lands, the consistent use of wine in religious ceremonies connected them to shared traditions.

15.4.2 Christianity

Wine is central to Christian rituals, particularly the **Eucharist** (also known as Communion or the Lord's Supper). In the New Testament, wine represents the blood of Christ, recalling Jesus's Last Supper. Different denominations have varied practices—some use real wine, others grape juice—but the symbolism of wine as a holy element is longstanding.

In the early Church, monks and priests cultivated vineyards to ensure a reliable wine supply for Mass. Over centuries, monastic orders like Benedictines and Cistercians refined wine production to fulfill religious needs. Christian festivals and feasts often included wine as part of fellowship meals, and many saints' days were celebrated with communal toasts, bridging liturgical and social joy.

15.4.3 Islam and Contrasting Views

Islam typically prohibits alcoholic beverages, viewing intoxication as harmful to spiritual discipline. Yet, references to wine appear in Islamic poetry and in mystical Sufi writings as a metaphor for divine love. Historically, some Islamic societies tolerated wine production if it was for non-Muslim communities or for medicinal reasons. In regions like Al-Andalus (Muslim Spain), Jewish and Christian minorities produced wine, and certain leaders turned a blind eye to limited local consumption.

However, official religious ceremonies in Islamic tradition do not include wine. Instead, believers focus on water or other non-alcoholic beverages for communal or festive occasions. This divergence from other religions underscores how faith shapes attitudes toward wine.

15.4.4 Hinduism, Buddhism, and Other Faiths

In Hinduism, alcoholic drinks (including wine if available) may be offered in certain rites to specific deities, though this is less common than in Mediterranean traditions. Some rural folk customs might use local fermented drinks in worship, but strict Hindu sects discourage alcohol. Similarly, many Buddhists, especially monks, avoid alcohol to maintain mental clarity, though certain local traditions might incorporate mild fermented beverages. Overall, wine plays a smaller role in these faiths' formal ceremonies compared to Christianity or Judaism.

15.5 Seasonal Festivals and Secular Celebrations

15.5.1 Harvest Festivals

For winegrowing regions, the harvest season is a time of great celebration. Ancient and medieval communities held harvest feasts, thanking gods or saints for a successful grape crop. People drank new wine or partially fermented must (sometimes called "vin bourru" in parts of France or "federweißer" in Germany). This practice continues in many places to this day, though we focus here on historical times, noting that harvest festivals have ancient roots.

In medieval Europe, local lords or monasteries might hold a feast for vineyard workers after a good harvest, sharing wine and food as a communal reward. Processions, music, and dancing could mark the end of the grape-picking season. These events reinforced community bonds and recognized the labor that went into creating wine.

15.5.2 Weddings and Social Milestones

Wine has traditionally been a key element in weddings, toasting the newly married couple. In ancient Greece, the bride and groom sometimes drank from a shared cup to symbolize unity. Roman weddings included a ritual libation to the gods, asking for blessings.

In many cultures, wine appears at coming-of-age ceremonies or other rites of passage, such as a boy's or girl's transition to adulthood. Historical accounts from various societies mention offering a ceremonial cup of wine to a new adult, acknowledging their entrance into community responsibilities.

15.5.3 Banquets, Feasts, and Court Ceremonies

Throughout history, banquets at royal courts or among the noble classes were lavish affairs that showcased power, generosity, and culture. Wine flowed freely at these events, served alongside multi-course meals. Such feasts might honor victorious generals, diplomatic visitors, or religious festivals. In medieval Europe, for example, the coronation of a king often ended with a grand feast where wine was poured from ornate vessels.

As the Renaissance advanced, courts like those of the Medici in Florence or the Valois in France further refined banquet customs, pairing wines with dishes and using these gatherings to display wealth and sophistication. Musicians, poets, and entertainers performed while guests sipped from fine goblets, toasting alliances or celebrating achievements.

15.6 Mourning and Memorial Ceremonies

15.6.1 Wine in Funerals

Wine is not just for joyful occasions—it also appears in funerary rites. As far back as ancient Egypt or Mesopotamia, wine was placed in tombs for the dead's afterlife journey. In Greek and Roman traditions, mourners sometimes poured wine over graves or cremation pyres to honor the deceased's spirit.

In Christian contexts, funeral wakes or vigils often included wine for consolation and as a communal act of remembering the departed. In some places, special toasts recalled the deceased's life. This blend of sorrow and ritual drinking helped communities process grief collectively.

15.6.2 Offerings to Ancestors

In certain cultures, wine offerings to ancestors continue at designated altars or shrines. In ancient China, while grain-based spirits were more common, fermented beverages sometimes included fruit wines, used in ceremonies to remember and honor family lines. The principle is similar across many traditions: wine, as a valuable liquid, symbolizes respect when shared with those who came before.

15.7 Symbolism and Meaning in Ritual Use

15.7.1 Wine as Transformation

Across cultures, wine often symbolizes a shift—from life to death, from sorrow to joy, or from mortal to divine realms. Fermentation itself is a transformation, turning grape juice into an intoxicating drink. Ancient myths connected this transformation to the cycle of life and rebirth. The Greek god Dionysus famously "died and was reborn," mirroring the grapevine's seasonal cycle. Wine ceremonies thus became metaphors for renewal and hope.

15.7.2 Purification and Blessing

In some rites, a small pour of wine on the ground purifies the space or invites blessings. This libation tradition existed in Greek, Roman,

Egyptian, and many other societies. Even in modern echoes of historical practice (though we focus on older times), people might "pour one out" in memory of someone or something important. In ancient contexts, the wine's color (especially red) was linked to vitality or life force.

15.7.3 Wine as a Unifying Element

Ceremonial wine fosters unity. Whether sipped by a congregation at a Christian Eucharist, shared at a wedding toast, or consumed at a Greek symposium, wine acts as a communal thread. People gather, drink together, and reinforce bonds or shared beliefs. This communal aspect has persisted throughout history, enabling wine to transcend its role as mere refreshment and become a symbol of shared identity.

15.8 Adaptations and Regional Variations

15.8.1 Middle Ages in Europe

In medieval Europe, the Church dominated many aspects of culture. Wine, central to the Mass, also became integral to major festivals—Easter, Christmas, saints' days, or local patron days. Religious processions sometimes included carrying wine barrels as offerings. Pilgrims traveling to holy sites might consume wine at hostels run by monks.

Nobles also developed secular celebrations, mixing feudal tradition with Christian rites. A knight's victory might be celebrated with a "wine feast," or a local lord might declare a wine-tasting day for his subjects on special occasions. Each region had its own flair: German communities along the Rhine might hold a spring festival with newly pressed wine, while in France's Champagne region, local fairs sometimes featured the latest sparkling experiments.

15.8.2 Renaissance and Beyond

During the Renaissance, humanist ideals led some thinkers to explore wine's links to creativity and intellectual discourse, reminiscent of ancient Greek symposia. Courts in Italy, France, and elsewhere refined the art of entertainment—pairing wines, planning masked balls, or staging elaborate theatrical presentations. While the direct influence of religion persisted, the Renaissance allowed a more secular approach to celebrations, where wine symbolized cultural sophistication as much as devotion.

In the Age of Exploration (15th–17th centuries) and the following centuries, wine-based ceremonies also traveled abroad. Catholic missionaries introduced the Mass with wine to the Americas, Africa, and Asia. Local adaptations occurred, where indigenous communities might blend old rites with newly introduced wine traditions, though this mix varied widely and sometimes clashed with local beliefs.

15.8.3 Non-Mediterranean Cultures

In regions where grapes did not grow well—like northern Europe or large parts of Asia—imported wine might still be used for certain high-status ceremonies. Courts in Russia, for example, served imported wines at grand feasts from the 17th century onward. In Japan's historical encounters with European traders, wine was sometimes offered as a diplomatic gift, although sake remained the primary ceremonial drink.

15.9 Decline or Persistence Over Time

15.9.1 Impact of Historical Shifts

Major changes—like the Reformation in Europe—sometimes reduced wine's ceremonial role in certain Protestant traditions, replacing it with simpler forms of communion or even with grape juice in specific groups (though that occurred mainly later). Likewise, wars, invasions, or economic downturns could disrupt wine production, making ceremonial wine scarce. However, the symbolic power of wine typically endured. People found ways to preserve essential rituals, sometimes resorting to other fermented beverages if wine was unavailable.

15.9.2 The Cultural Memory of Wine Ceremonies

Even when societies modernized or faced adversity (plagues, invasions, etc.), they tended to keep core wine traditions. For example, in Jewish communities scattered by diaspora, the Sabbath Kiddush wine ritual remained a constant link to identity. In Christian Europe, the Eucharist continued despite political upheavals, reconfirming wine's place in worship. Over centuries, these customs fed into a deep cultural memory, so that even in times of shortage or prohibition, wine's ceremonial significance remained powerful.

CHAPTER 16

Understanding Historical Grape Varieties

16.1 Introduction

Grapevines come in countless varieties, each with its own flavor profile, growing habit, and adaptability to soil and climate. While today we recognize famous names like Cabernet Sauvignon, Chardonnay, or Pinot Noir, many old varieties once flourished in ancient vineyards, and some have vanished over time. Others persist in limited regions, representing living links to centuries of wine heritage.

In this chapter, we will explore historical grape varieties from ancient times through the 19th century. We will see how cultures named, classified, and sometimes revered certain grapes, how these vines spread along trade routes, and how local preferences shaped which grapes thrived. We will also discuss how early ampelographers (people who study grapevines) tried to record and categorize varieties, and how the arrival of phylloxera forced a reevaluation of which grapes were worth saving. By the end, you will understand how today's well-known grapes are just part of a grand tapestry of vine diversity that stretches back thousands of years.

16.2 Ancient Grape Varieties in the Near East and the Mediterranean

16.2.1 Beginnings in the Caucasus and Fertile Crescent

Archaeological evidence points to the Caucasus region (modern-day Georgia, Armenia) and nearby areas (eastern Turkey, northern Iran) as the cradle of early grape domestication. Wild vines (Vitis vinifera subsp. sylvestris) gradually gave rise to cultivated forms (Vitis vinifera subsp. vinifera). While we lack precise names for these prehistoric strains, ancient seeds and DNA analyses suggest a diversity of vines.

As wine became a staple in the Fertile Crescent, local farmers selected vines that produced reliable yields or pleasing flavors. Over generations, these early cultivars spread through trade and migration into Egypt, Mesopotamia, and beyond. Textual records from Sumerian or Babylonian tablets occasionally mention vineyards, but rarely specify grape types beyond simple descriptors like "red" or "sweet."

16.2.2 Egypt and the Levant

Egyptian tomb scenes and wall inscriptions show red and white grape clusters, but do not name distinct varieties. Nonetheless, some scientists have studied seeds from tombs, finding morphological differences that hint at multiple grape types. The Levant (encompassing modern Lebanon, Israel/Palestine, Syria) developed a wine culture that may have included early forms of grapes like those still grown in the region (for example, certain indigenous varieties in Lebanon).

Ancient Phoenicians (from the Levant coast) were notable seafarers who carried vines and wine knowledge across the Mediterranean, establishing links to North Africa, Sicily, and southern Spain. Over centuries, their trade likely contributed to the spread of varieties that evolved into local strains.

16.2.3 Greece and Early Ampelography

In ancient Greece, people recognized that not all grapes were the same. Certain regions were famed for strong, sweet wines (like those from Chios or Thasos). Though the Greeks did not systematically list varieties as we do today, references in texts by Homer or later authors mention special vines prized for taste or medicinal properties. Dionysus, the wine god, was sometimes credited with teaching humans about cultivating specific grapes.

Greek colonists carried cuttings to southern Italy, Sicily, and along the Black Sea coasts. These transplantations introduced Greek-origin grapes to local soils, where they adapted and evolved. Though we cannot be certain which modern grapes descend from those lines, many Mediterranean vines trace partial lineage to Greek settlers.

16.2.4 Rome: Falernian and Others

The Romans expanded vine cultivation extensively, recording some early ampelographic observations. Writers like Pliny the Elder, Columella, and Varro wrote about famous wines such as **Falernian**, **Caecuban**, and others. Falernian was often described as a high-quality white or amber wine from the slopes near Mount Falernus (in Campania). Though the exact grape behind Falernian is lost, it might have been related to today's varieties grown in Campania (like Greco or Falanghina).

Romans noted different vine characteristics: early ripening vs. late ripening, sweet must vs. dry. They recognized that vines from one region transplanted elsewhere might change in quality. Roman amphora stamps sometimes named the vineyard or region but rarely gave a grape name. Even so, their broad expansion across Europe laid the groundwork for many local grape populations that persisted into medieval times.

16.3 Medieval and Monastic Contributions

16.3.1 Monasteries as Vine Guardians

After the fall of the Western Roman Empire, monastic communities preserved vine cultivation, ensuring wine supply for religious ceremonies. Monks in regions like Burgundy, the Rhine Valley, and parts of Italy became keen observers of vineyard differences. They might notice that grapes from one hillside produced richer wine than from another. Over centuries, this led to the concept of vineyard terroir—though formal naming of the vines themselves was still loose.

Some medieval monastic records mention grapes by color (blanc, noir, gris) or by local place names (like "the vine from the hillside near the abbey"). Over time, distinctive vines gained local nicknames. Yet a single variety could bear multiple names across different villages, causing confusion. In Burgundy, for example, Pinot Noir became a dominant red grape, though it might have had local synonyms or close kin that the monks noticed but did not systematically label.

16.3.2 The Emergence of Named Medieval Varieties

In certain medieval documents, a few grape names appear:

- **Gamay**: Found in Burgundy, known for producing abundant yields.
- **Muscat**: Valued for its aromatic grapes, grown in the Mediterranean.
- **Malvasia** (Malvagia, Malmsey): A family of grapes that produce sweet, heady wines, associated with the eastern Mediterranean.

These names typically referred to broader families rather than precise, single "clonal" varieties. The fluid naming environment reflected the era's limited scientific approach—people recognized differences but lacked a standardized classification system.

16.3.3 Local Adaptations

European regions that had once grown Roman-era vines now had centuries of local evolution. Climate shifts (like the Medieval Warm Period) allowed certain grapes to thrive farther north than before.

Monasteries selected hardy vines well-suited to each microclimate. Some vines traveled with monastic orders—for instance, Cistercians who established daughter houses in distant lands, bringing cuttings from their mother abbey's prized grapes.

16.4 Renaissance and Early Modern Observations

16.4.1 Travel and Grape Exchange

During the Renaissance, renewed trade and exploration exposed vineyard owners to foreign grape types. Italian city-states like Venice or Genoa might receive Greek or Middle Eastern vines. Spanish explorers brought cuttings to the Americas. However, official naming remained inconsistent, and many grape shipments were described in general terms: "We brought a sweet white vine from Crete" or "We carried a black grape from Cyprus."

Certain noble courts took special interest in exotic vines. A wealthy landowner might plant foreign grapes in a demonstration vineyard, seeking novel flavors. Over time, some of these experimental plantings adapted to local conditions, eventually becoming integrated into the region's vine population.

16.4.2 Early Ampelographers

By the 16th and 17th centuries, a few scholars tried to systematically describe plants, including grapevines. Botanists like Pietro de' Crescenzi in Italy or later works in Central Europe included sections on viticulture. They would note leaf shapes, berry colors, and wine characteristics, though their descriptions were often broad and lacked modern precision.

These writers laid the groundwork for the 18th and 19th centuries, when more formal classification efforts arose. In France, a figure like

Antoine de Jussieu (an 18th-century botanist) might dabble in describing vines, but a fully developed ampelographic science would wait for the 19th century.

16.5 The 18th and Early 19th Centuries: Toward Classification

16.5.1 Rising Interest in Specific Grapes

As discussed in earlier chapters, the 18th century saw growing demand for wine among middle classes and connoisseurs. People began to identify which regions—and, by extension, which grapes—produced superior wines. Bordeaux gained renown for its blends based largely on Cabernet Sauvignon, Merlot, and others. Burgundy took pride in Pinot Noir and Chardonnay. The Rhine Valley championed Riesling. However, each region had multiple local cultivars, with only the most famous ones recognized beyond local borders.

In Spain, grapes like **Palomino** (for Sherry) and **Tempranillo** (under various local names) started to be singled out. In Portugal, the **Touriga** family was recognized for making robust Port wines. Meanwhile, in Italy, local names abounded: Sangiovese, Nebbiolo, Aglianico, etc. But these were only glimpses; many other minor grapes remained hidden in rural vineyards, known only to local farmers.

16.5.2 Early Grapevine Studies

Some wealthy estate owners in France, Germany, or Austria financed small-scale studies of grape types. They might gather cuttings from different provinces, plant them side by side, and observe differences. These were often private efforts, not widely published, but they contributed to a growing sense that grape variety—alongside soil and climate—shaped wine character.

By the early 19th century, certain wine merchants also recognized that specifying the grape could help marketing. For instance, a merchant might note that a wine was predominantly "Pineau noir" (an older term related to Pinot Noir) or "Carbene-Sauvignon" (an archaic spelling for Cabernet Sauvignon). These naming attempts were still inconsistent, but laid a foundation for modern labeling.

16.5.3 American Vines and the Old World

In the colonial period, North American vines (like Vitis labrusca, Vitis rotundifolia, etc.) were tested in Europe, but rarely embraced for wine production due to their distinct "foxy" flavors. Europeans were primarily interested in these vines for rootstock experiments, especially once phylloxera became a threat in the later 19th century. However, in the early 1800s, the link between American vines and phylloxera resistance was not yet fully recognized, so American vines remained curiosities rather than mainstream cultivars.

16.6 The Phylloxera Crisis and Its Effect on Grape Diversity

16.6.1 Mass Replanting

As covered in Chapter 14, phylloxera in the late 19th century forced Europeans to uproot and replant millions of vines. When replanting on American rootstocks, many growers chose more commercially viable or well-known varieties, shrinking the presence of lesser-known local grapes. This inadvertently reduced biodiversity, as older or lower-yielding vines were replaced with "safer bets."

16.6.2 Hybrid Grapes

Along with grafting, some breeders created **hybrid grapes** by crossing American and European vines. Their goal was to get phylloxera resistance and better disease tolerance while retaining decent flavor. Many of these hybrids never achieved top wine quality (by European taste standards), but they thrived in regions with harsh climates or poor soils. Though some hybrids found success in certain corners of Europe, the mainstream preference still favored traditional Vitis vinifera scions on American roots.

16.6.3 Ampelographic Efforts

The phylloxera crisis fueled an urgent need to identify valuable European grapes worth saving. Ampelographers cataloged vines, noting leaf shapes, cluster forms, berry color, and typical wine profiles. Notable 19th-century researchers like Victor Pulliat in France or Hermann Goethe in Austria published early lists of recognized varieties. This systematic approach helped preserve some diversity that might have been lost in the scramble to replant.

16.7 Examples of Historical Grape Varieties

Below, we highlight a few grapes with deep historical roots, acknowledging that countless others shaped local wines across centuries.

16.7.1 Pinot Noir (France)

Pinot Noir's history dates back at least to medieval Burgundy, where Cistercian monks championed it. Some legends claim it is over 1,000 years old as a cultivated variety. Renowned for producing delicate, complex reds, Pinot Noir spread to Champagne (for sparkling wines) and beyond. In old texts, it might appear as Morillon or Noirien, reflecting local naming quirks.

16.7.2 Nebbiolo (Italy)

Nebbiolo, grown in Piedmont (northwestern Italy), is the backbone of famous Barolo and Barbaresco wines today. Historic references to

Nebbiolo-like grapes appear in documents from the 13th–14th centuries. The name possibly comes from "nebbia" (fog) or "noble," though historians debate. Medieval records show that local lords prized this grape for strong, aromatic wines.

16.7.3 Palomino (Spain)

Palomino is central to Sherry production in Jerez, Spain. It likely has roots in Iberian vineyards dating to ancient or early medieval times. By the 16th–17th centuries, references to Palomino emerged in local archives describing its suitability for fortified wines. Over centuries, it adapted to the chalky "albariza" soils of southern Spain, becoming the region's hallmark white grape.

16.7.4 Xynisteri (Cyprus)

In the eastern Mediterranean, indigenous grapes like **Xynisteri** have long histories. Cyprus has produced wine for millennia, with references going back to classical times. By medieval and Renaissance eras, travelers mentioned sweet Cypriot wines. Xynisteri likely contributed to these wines, though exact historical names can be tricky to trace. Still, it is a survivor from an ancient lineage of local grapes.

16.7.5 Mission Grape (Listán Prieto) in the Americas

Spanish colonists brought **Listán Prieto** from the Canary Islands to the New World in the 16th century. Known as the Mission grape in California or País in Chile, it formed the backbone of early colonial wine production. Though not originally "New World," it adapted to soils in Mexico, Peru, Chile, and beyond. Its presence across vast colonial territories underscores how one variety can shape multiple wine cultures.

16.8 Naming Confusion and Local Synonyms

16.8.1 Synonyms Galore

One grape might have dozens of synonyms across Europe. For instance, **Tempranillo** in Spain is called Tinta Roriz in Portugal's Douro region and Cencibel in La Mancha. **Garnacha** in Spain is **Grenache** in France, **Cannonau** in Sardinia, and so on. Historically, local farmers named vines for color, shape, or a village. Without standardized nomenclature, confusion ran rampant.

16.8.2 Attempts at Standardization

During the 19th century, some horticultural societies tried to unify names by publishing reference guides. Yet, differences in dialect and historical usage persisted. It was only in the 20th century (outside our primary timeframe) that large-scale genetic testing and international wine commerce gradually aligned naming conventions. Still, the 19th-century beginnings of these efforts laid important groundwork.

16.8.3 Importance of Local Identity

Despite confusion, local synonyms also reflect the cultural significance of grapes in each region's heritage. Farmers who prided themselves on a unique local vine name were perpetuating centuries of tradition. This sense of identity helped keep diverse varieties alive, even as more famous grapes dominated commerce.

16.9 Cultural and Historical Significance

16.9.1 Grapes as a Symbol of Regional Pride

Certain grapes became emblems of a region's identity. For instance, Sangiovese in Tuscany or Riesling along the Rhine served as cultural cornerstones. They appeared in local songs, legends, or folk art.

Medieval feasts might highlight a region's special grape variety to impress visiting dignitaries. Over time, these associations grew so strong that the variety's success or failure mattered to the region's economy and prestige.

16.9.2 Influence on Wine Styles

Differences among grape varieties shaped historical wine styles. A sweet, late-harvest Muscat might be revered in one area for dessert wines, while a robust Nebbiolo in Piedmont produced structured reds for aging. By medieval or Renaissance times, some cities specialized in certain wine categories, exporting them widely. This interplay between variety and style fueled trade routes, alliances, and occasionally conflicts over wine pricing or taxes.

16.9.3 Preservation and Loss

Over centuries, certain grapes vanished due to wars, disease, changing tastes, or political upheavals. The phylloxera crisis accelerated these losses, as replanting costs pushed growers toward "safe," profitable choices. Yet some ancient varieties survived, kept alive by dedicated farmers or remote hillside communities. Their continued existence offers living proof of how historical grapes can endure against the odds, preserving a tangible link to the past.

CHAPTER 17

Wine in Art and Literature Through History

17.1 Introduction

From the earliest cave drawings to the grand canvases of the Renaissance and the poetic verses of many cultures, wine has been an enduring subject for creative minds. Artists and writers have captured its color, symbolism, and social significance. They have used wine as a metaphor for love, life, and even divine inspiration.

In this chapter, we will examine how wine has appeared in different forms of art and literature across many centuries, focusing on pre-modern times. We will start with ancient depictions in sculpture and pottery, move through medieval illuminations and religious references, and explore the poetic and theatrical works of influential authors. We will see how wine served as a muse—an inspiration for creativity—and also as a reflection of social customs. Along the way, we will catch a glimpse of how changing attitudes toward wine shaped, and were shaped by, the art and writing that celebrated it.

17.2 Ancient World: Visual Representations and Early Literature

17.2.1 Cave Art and Early Symbolism

While most prehistoric cave art focuses on animals or hunting scenes, it's possible that some early depictions of grape clusters or simple plant outlines represented the importance of wild grapes.

Hard evidence is scarce, but the idea that grapes and wine might appear in rudimentary art suggests that humans recognized wine's special place early on.

In regions like the Caucasus or the Fertile Crescent, shards of pottery from Neolithic times sometimes carry designs that could be interpreted as vines or grape motifs. Such symbolic portrayals might have signified the cultural importance of wine, though the exact messages remain speculative.

17.2.2 Mesopotamia and Egypt

Moving into recorded history, we see more concrete evidence. Mesopotamian cylinder seals and relief carvings occasionally show feasts or offerings of wine. Artwork in royal palaces or temple contexts highlights the role of wine in religious rites, with priests and kings depicted pouring libations.

In ancient Egypt, tomb wall paintings are famous for showing grape harvesting and wine-making scenes. The artistry is detailed, capturing workers picking grapes, stomping them, and filling jars. These images not only served a decorative purpose but also ensured that the deceased would have access to wine in the afterlife. Egyptian hieroglyphs sometimes depicted jars with a short text about the vineyard's location or the year of a pharaoh's reign, foreshadowing later labeling practices.

17.2.3 Greek Pottery and Dionysian Imagery

The ancient Greeks used painted pottery—amphorae, kraters, kylixes—to depict mythological and everyday scenes. Many vases show Dionysus, the god of wine, accompanied by satyrs or maenads in revelry. The black-figure or red-figure styles often include swirling vines or motifs referencing wine's cultural importance.

Greek literature abounds with references to wine. Homer's epics (*The Iliad* and *The Odyssey*) describe wine as a prized resource, sometimes stored in large jars and offered to guests to show hospitality. Poets like Hesiod and later lyric poets included praise of wine's pleasures. The Greek theatrical tradition, especially comedies and satyr plays, also used wine as a theme or prop, illustrating both its positive social role and its potential for chaos.

17.2.4 Roman Frescoes and Writings

Romans, inheriting Greek traditions, depicted wine in frescoes on the walls of villas, showing banquet scenes or Bacchic rites. The city of Pompeii, buried by Mount Vesuvius in 79 CE, offers a vivid snapshot: many houses had dining rooms with painted walls celebrating abundance and wine. Mosaics sometimes featured grape clusters or comedic references to inebriation.

Roman literature is equally rich. Writers like Virgil, Horace, and Ovid sang the praises of wine. Horace's odes include lines about the joy of drinking a fine Falernian vintage or sharing a cup among friends. Meanwhile, comedic dramatists used drunk characters to create humorous or moral lessons, reflecting wine's double-sided nature—pleasure and potential vice.

17.3 Medieval and Renaissance Interpretations

17.3.1 Illuminated Manuscripts and Symbolic Use

During the Middle Ages, much of Europe's literacy and artistic production were centered in monasteries. Illuminated manuscripts, especially biblical texts, sometimes featured wine motifs. Marginal decorations could show small vines or tiny scenes of grape harvest, linking wine to religious themes (like the Eucharist) and acknowledging its everyday role.

In Christian art, scenes of the Last Supper and the Crucifixion often included references to wine, symbolizing Christ's blood. The vine itself became a powerful Christian symbol: Jesus referred to himself as the "true vine" in the Gospels, so medieval artists used vine imagery to represent spiritual life and unity. Stained glass windows in cathedrals occasionally depicted biblical parables involving vineyards.

17.3.2 Epic Poetry and Courtly Literature

Medieval poets and troubadours composed verses extolling wine as part of courtly life. In chivalric romances, feasts where wine was served demonstrated a castle's hospitality. Arthurian legends might mention knights drinking wine at King Arthur's table, though mead or ale also appeared. In the French epic *The Song of Roland*, references to wine highlight wealth and camaraderie among warriors.

Secular medieval art often portrayed banquets with fine foods and wine, symbolizing abundance or celebrating key moments like coronations or victory feasts. Tapestries, for example, might show vineyard scenes to underscore a noble family's holdings and prosperity.

17.3.3 Renaissance Painting and Literary Flourish

The Renaissance propelled wine imagery into new realms of sophistication. Painters in Italy, Flanders, and beyond used more realistic techniques to depict banquets, harvests, and mythological scenes. Dionysian motifs reemerged in a classical revival, with figures like Bacchus or fauns featured in luscious, pastoral settings.

Artists such as Titian, Caravaggio, and Veronese painted grand banquet or Bacchic scenes, capturing the opulence of wine jugs, elaborate goblets, and the interplay of light on grapes. Meanwhile, Renaissance humanists, influenced by classical literature, praised wine as a stimulant for intellectual discourse. Writers like Rabelais in France used wine references comically and philosophically, while in Elizabethan England, Shakespeare's plays frequently mention wine or sack (sherry), reflecting the era's lively drinking culture.

17.4 Baroque to Enlightenment: Shifting Styles

17.4.1 Still-Life Paintings

From the 17th century onward, still-life painting became a major genre, especially in the Low Countries (today's Netherlands and Belgium) and Spain. Artists like Jan Davidsz. de Heem or Francisco de Zurbarán created sumptuous displays of fruit, flowers, and vessels of wine. These paintings emphasized both the beauty and transience of earthly pleasures—wine included.

In Dutch still-lifes (or pronk still-lifes), a half-filled glass of wine symbolized fleeting luxury, often paired with a skull or wilting flower to hint at life's brevity. Spanish bodegones, or kitchen scenes, sometimes included a jug or wineskin, underscoring humble daily realities. These contrasts—lavish vs. humble—show how artists used wine to reflect moral and social commentary.

17.4.2 Theater and Satire

The Baroque and early Enlightenment periods saw plays and poems that ridiculed drunkenness or praised moderate enjoyment. Molière's comedies occasionally featured wine-fueled misunderstandings, while English Restoration playwrights included tipsy aristocrats to highlight moral flaws or comedic chaos.

Poets of the era, such as John Dryden or Alexander Pope, might reference wine in passing, linking it to convivial gatherings or witty repartee. Similarly, Spain's Golden Age dramatists (like Calderón de la Barca) sometimes used wine as a stage device—accidentally spilled wine might trigger comedic revelations, or a character's drunken rant might reveal hidden truths.

17.5 Romanticism and Beyond

17.5.1 Poetic Reveries

The Romantic movement (late 18th–early 19th century) elevated emotions, nature, and individual experience. Poets such as Johann Wolfgang von Goethe in Germany or Lord Byron in England wrote about the intensity of feeling—love, despair, ecstasy—and often included references to wine as a symbol of passion or creative fury.

In French literature, Alphonse de Lamartine or Victor Hugo occasionally used wine imagery to describe fleeting happiness or communal solidarity. Many Romantic writers, enthralled by the classical past, evoked Bacchic festivals or used wine to represent liberation from societal constraints. Yet they also acknowledged the darker side of indulgence, hinting at wine's capacity to reveal hidden depths of the soul.

17.5.2 Folklore and National Identity

As 19th-century nationalism grew, writers and artists sought local traditions. Wine regions—like the Rhine in Germany or the Douro in Portugal—became romanticized in landscape paintings and folk tales. German poets, for instance, wrote about Rhine wine festivals, weaving them into patriotic expressions of cultural heritage. Portuguese authors celebrated vineyard terraces carved into hillsides, linking them to national pride.

In Eastern Europe, traveling minstrels or bards might compose songs celebrating local wines. Such ballads, retold in writing, fused wine with stories of heroism, love, or communal unity. These narratives helped define a region's cultural identity and often remain part of traditional lore.

17.6 Religious and Moral Themes in Art and Literature

17.6.1 Christian Motifs

Throughout history, Christian art depicted wine in scenes of the Last Supper or Eucharist, signifying Christ's sacrifice. Medieval, Renaissance, and Baroque masters included chalices or references to vineyards as coded symbols of salvation. From Giotto's frescoes to Caravaggio's dramatic chiaroscuro, the chalice of wine is a recurring motif for divine love or redemption.

Sermons and religious texts also used wine allegorically. For example, monastic writers might compare the spiritual life to a vineyard needing careful cultivation and pruning. These literary metaphors reinforced the religious significance of wine beyond the physical drink.

17.6.2 Moral Lessons and Temperance

Alongside celebratory art, some works carried warnings about excessive drinking. Woodcuts from the 16th–18th centuries might illustrate the "Stages of Drunkenness," depicting how a person's dignity crumbled with each cup. Writers from moral or religious backgrounds penned pamphlets cautioning about the perils of overindulgence.

In Protestant regions of Northern Europe, such didactic art and texts grew more common, reflecting a cultural emphasis on moderation. A painting might show a well-dressed man turning into a brawling figure after too much wine, highlighting a moral downfall. These cautionary tales show that while wine was admired, society also recognized its dangers if misused.

17.7 Wine in Non-Western Art and Literature

17.7.1 Middle Eastern Poetry

In Islamic culture, the Qur'an prohibits the consumption of alcohol, yet classical Persian poets like Hafez or Omar Khayyam extensively used wine as a metaphor for spiritual ecstasy, love, or divine union. Their verses describe wine's color, fragrance, and the intoxication of the soul. Though literal wine-drinking was typically frowned upon, the symbolic "wine" in Sufi or Persian poetry soared with philosophical and mystical significance.

These poetic traditions influenced art forms like Persian miniature painting, which occasionally depicted banquets or gatherings in historical or mythological settings, sometimes with wine present. Scholars debate how literal these images and poems were versus purely symbolic.

17.7.2 Chinese and Japanese Art

In East Asia, grain-based beverages like rice wine (sake) or huangjiu dominated. Still, grape wine did appear in some contexts, especially along the Silk Road or in imperial courts that imported exotic goods. Ancient Chinese poets—such as Li Bai of the Tang Dynasty—mentioned "wine" in verse, though often referring to rice wine. However, some references might blend the concept of fermented drink generally.

Artworks might depict banquets with officials or scholars drinking from cups, though the beverage was more likely a grain-based spirit. Even so, the notion of drinking to spur poetic inspiration was strong in Chinese culture. Over centuries, travelers returning from Central Asia brought occasional references to grape-based wine. Such influences remained limited but highlight how wine's symbolic weight transcended purely Western traditions.

17.8 The Late 19th-Century Evolution

17.8.1 Realist and Impressionist Art

By the late 19th century, Realist and Impressionist movements in Europe often depicted everyday life, including cafés and bars where wine or absinthe might be served. Painters like Édouard Manet or Edgar Degas portrayed Parisian café scenes, sometimes focusing on the lonely or reflective drinker. While these are more modern glimpses, they trace back to historical attitudes about social drinking.

In more rural landscapes, artists might show grape harvesters or vineyard vistas, celebrating agricultural traditions. Again, while tipping slightly into the modern era, these paintings echo centuries of harvest imagery found in older manuscripts and classical art.

17.8.2 Literary Movements and Symbolists

Late 19th-century writers, especially Symbolists like Charles Baudelaire or Paul Verlaine, used wine to evoke altered states of mind. Baudelaire's *Les Fleurs du mal* includes poems addressing intoxication as a metaphor for transcending mundane reality. These works, while modern in approach, remain rooted in ancient traditions that link wine to creativity and spiritual seeking.

CHAPTER 18

Notable Historical Wine Regions (Up to the 19th Century)

18.1 Introduction

Wine is a product of place—each region's soil, climate, and culture combine to create distinct styles. Over centuries, certain regions rose to fame because their wines excelled in quality, trade advantage, or royal patronage. Some garnered recognition from ancient empires; others found prominence later through monastic stewardship or the tastes of powerful courts.

In this chapter, we will explore major wine-growing regions across Europe and beyond, focusing on their development up to the 19th century. We will see how geography, politics, and local traditions shaped unique wine cultures in areas like Bordeaux, Burgundy, Champagne, the Rhine, Tokaj, Jerez, the Douro, and others. We will also touch on key regions in the Mediterranean, the New World colonies, and how each found its identity before modern industrial changes. Through these regions, we gain a comprehensive view of how wine turned from a local beverage into an international force that influenced economies, social customs, and culinary practices.

18.2 France: A Patchwork of Renowned Terroirs

18.2.1 Bordeaux

Location & Early History: Bordeaux, in southwestern France, lies along the Garonne and Dordogne Rivers, forming the Gironde estuary. Romans introduced vines, and the region flourished under medieval English rule (following the marriage of Eleanor of Aquitaine to King Henry II). Exports of "claret" to England cemented its reputation.

Development & Key Grapes: By the 17th–18th centuries, Bordeaux merchants expanded, draining marshes in the Médoc to create new vineyards. Grapes like Cabernet Sauvignon, Merlot, and Cabernet Franc became the backbone of red blends. The region also produced sweet whites in Sauternes (notably Château d'Yquem) and dry whites in Graves.

Prestige & Trade: British and Dutch traders propelled Bordeaux to global fame, establishing négociant networks. By the early 19th century, certain châteaux were recognized as consistently superior, setting the stage for the 1855 Classification (though that formal ranking is outside our main timeline). Even so, Bordeaux had earned an elite status well before then.

18.2.2 Burgundy

Location & Origins: Stretching from Chablis down through the Côte d'Or to the Mâconnais, Burgundy traces vine roots back to Roman times. Monastic orders (Benedictines, then Cistercians) meticulously cultivated the land through the Middle Ages, noting differences among vineyard plots.

Pinot Noir and Chardonnay: Burgundy's red grape, Pinot Noir, and its white star, Chardonnay, came to define the region. The monks' detailed observations of terroir laid the groundwork for the concept of "climat" and "cru," referencing specific vineyard sites.

Fragmentation & Reputation: Post-French Revolution, vineyards were split among many owners. Yet the region's fame endured. By the 19th century, the Côte d'Or (divided into Côte de Nuits and Côte de Beaune) was already prized by royalty and connoisseurs for nuanced, age-worthy wines.

18.2.3 Champagne

Origins: This northern region of France historically produced still wines—often pale or slightly pinkish. The idea of deliberate sparkling wine only emerged around the 17th century. Early adopters like the Benedictine monk Dom Pérignon (d. 1715) refined methods, though the full industry take-off was more 18th–19th century.

Climate & Grapes: Champagne's cool climate challenged viticulture, but the chalky soils and low temperatures ultimately favored crisp, high-acid grapes such as Pinot Noir, Chardonnay, and Pinot Meunier. Sparkling production, aided by stronger glass bottles, found a niche among Europe's aristocracy.

Rise to Fame: Even before modern branding, Champagne was associated with royal coronations in Reims. By the late 18th and early 19th centuries, certain houses (Ruinart, Moët, Veuve Clicquot) gained renown for producing effervescent wine that symbolized luxury and celebration.

18.3 Iberian Peninsula: Spain and Portugal

18.3.1 Jerez (Sherry)

Location & History: The Jerez region in southwestern Spain boasts a long tradition, dating back to Phoenician times. Under Islamic rule (8th–15th centuries), wine production persisted for non-Muslim communities and medicinal purposes. After the Reconquista, Sherry's export soared.

Palomino & Fortification: By the 16th century, Sherry (called "sack" in Elizabethan England) was revered abroad. Palomino grapes flourish in the chalky albariza soils. Fortifying the wine with grape spirit helped it survive sea voyages, enhancing its appeal to foreign markets.

Solera System: Although fully developed in later centuries, an early version of the solera aging method—blending younger wine with older stocks—existed. By the 18th century, Sherry had a strong presence in British and colonial markets, shaping the region's commercial identity.

18.3.2 Rioja

Location & Influence: Northeastern Spain's Rioja sits along the Ebro River. Monasteries and pilgrims on the Camino de Santiago played a role in medieval vine expansion. Historically, local wines were overshadowed by Sherry's fame. But from the late 18th century, certain estates began adopting oak barrel aging, influenced by French techniques.

Tempranillo and Garnacha: Rioja's main grapes—Tempranillo, Garnacha (Grenache), Mazuelo (Carignan), Graciano—suited the region's varied soils and microclimates. Early forms of barrel maturation (though not fully standardized) gave Rioja wines more complexity.

Trade Connections: French merchants occasionally sourced Rioja wines when phylloxera damaged Bordeaux, bringing new recognition to the area. While true modernization came later, by the early 19th century, Rioja was positioning itself as a serious wine region.

18.3.3 The Douro (Port)

Geography & Early Fame: Northern Portugal's Douro Valley is rugged, with terraced vineyards carved into schist slopes. Romans introduced vines, but Port's distinct style emerged in the 17th century after British merchants sought alternative wine sources during Anglo-French conflicts.

Fortification & British Involvement: By the mid-18th century, adding brandy to arrest fermentation created sweet, robust Port. Major British wine companies (like Warre, Taylor, Graham) established lodges in Vila Nova de Gaia near Porto. Port shipments to England soared.

Regulation: The Marquis of Pombal set up one of the first regional wine regulations (1756), demarcating the Douro. By the 19th century, Port was well-known across Europe, though phylloxera later battered the valley, forcing replanting.

18.4 Central and Eastern Europe

18.4.1 The Rhine and Mosel (Germany)

Roman Beginnings: The Romans planted vines along the Rhine and its tributaries. Medieval monasteries expanded vineyards, focusing on steep, slate-laden slopes for crisp white wines.

Riesling & Others: By the 18th and early 19th centuries, Riesling was emerging as the signature grape of the Rhine and Mosel, valued for high acidity and age-worthy sweetness. Spätlese ("late harvest") or Auslese wines, discovered by chance, became prized for depth of flavor.

Trade & Reputation: Noble families and ecclesiastical estates refined winemaking, occasionally exporting to Britain, Scandinavia, or the Baltics. Germanic states' political fragmentation hindered a unified wine identity, but key regions like the Rheingau, Mosel-Saar-Ruwer, and Pfalz carved out reputations for elegant whites.

18.4.2 Tokaj (Hungary)

Early History: The Tokaj region in northeastern Hungary (historically part of the Habsburg Empire) found fame with its sweet

Aszú wines, derived from botrytized (noble rot) grapes. Vineyards were cultivated since medieval times, but the 17th century saw a rising profile for Tokaji.

Aszú Method: Grapes affected by Botrytis cinerea (called "aszú" in Hungarian) concentrated sugars. Winemakers added aszú paste to a base wine, creating luscious, honeyed beverages. This unique style attracted royal courts across Europe—"Tokaji Aszú" was prized by kings like Louis XIV of France, who allegedly called it "Vinum Regum, Rex Vinorum" (Wine of Kings, King of Wines).

Decline & Challenges: Wars and shifting political boundaries sometimes disrupted Tokaj's exports. Yet, by the early 19th century, Tokaji was recognized as one of Europe's great sweet wines, symbolizing Hungarian national heritage.

18.4.3 Austria and Bohemia

Regions & Grape Varieties: Austrian regions like Wachau, Kremstal, and Kamptal along the Danube also trace viticulture to Roman times. Monasteries preserved knowledge, cultivating grapes such as Grüner Veltliner (though it wasn't singled out in name until later) and Riesling. Bohemia and Moravia (Czech lands) also had smaller vineyards, particularly for local consumption.

Habsburg Influence: Under the Habsburg monarchy, cross-cultural exchange with Hungary and other territories introduced new vines and methods. However, many wines remained regional or for imperial courts, seldom gaining the broad export profile of French or Iberian wines.

18.5 The Italian Peninsula

18.5.1 Tuscany

Roman Legacy & Middle Ages: Tuscany's rolling hills around Florence and Siena have a viticulture lineage stretching to the

Etruscans and Romans. Medieval city-states fostered local wine commerce, while monastic orders kept vineyards in good repair.

Sangiovese & Chianti: By the 18th century, references to a "Chianti" style wine appeared, based on Sangiovese grapes. The region became known for robust reds enjoyed by both local nobility and foreign travelers. Winemakers experimented with blends, though official regulations were not yet in place.

Economic Ties: Tuscan wines sold in Florence's markets, often carried in straw-covered flasks (fiaschi). British travelers on the Grand Tour might taste local vintages, writing about them in diaries and letters. This modest international interest paved the way for expanded reputation later.

18.5.2 Piedmont

Location & Grape Heritage: Northwestern Italy's Piedmont, nestled near the Alps, cultivated Nebbiolo, Barbera, and Dolcetto for centuries. Monasteries shaped early vineyard traditions. By the 19th century, certain local noble families, such as the House of Savoy, supported improvements in viticulture.

Nebbiolo Wines: Pre-1850 references to robust Nebbiolo-based wines show that Barolo and Barbaresco's ancestors were already respected, though not as widely famed as Bordeaux or Burgundy. Piedmontese growers worked with extended maceration and aging in casks, yielding structured red wines that gained recognition among aristocrats.

18.5.3 Southern Regions

Naples & Sicily: Southern Italy's volcanic soils around Vesuvius or on the island of Sicily gave rise to numerous indigenous grapes (Aglianico, Nero d'Avola, among others). Ancient fame for Falernian, grown near Campania, lingered through medieval times, though overshadowed by northern and central regions in international markets.

Export vs. Local Consumption: Many southern areas produced bulk wine for local drinking or for blending with lighter northern wines. Some sweet styles (like Marsala in Sicily) found export markets, especially with British merchants, echoing the pattern of other fortified wines.

18.6 The Eastern Mediterranean and Beyond

18.6.1 Greece and the Aegean

Despite ancient glory, by the Ottoman era (15th–19th centuries), Greek wine production faced restrictions. Certain islands (e.g., Santorini, Crete) continued local traditions, with sweet vinsanto or malvasia. Venetian or Genoese control in some regions also influenced local styles. Exports were modest, mostly to Venice or small markets, but the deep cultural memory of Dionysian heritage persisted.

18.6.2 Cyprus

Cyprus boasted a wine culture dating back to at least the Bronze Age. During medieval Crusader kingdoms, "Commandaria"—a sweet fortified wine—became famed in European courts. By the 18th century, production carried on under Ottoman rule with limited overseas trade, though local appreciation never waned.

18.6.3 The Levant and Ottoman Influence

Under Ottoman administration, large-scale commercial wine sales were restricted by Islamic law. However, Christian and Jewish communities in regions like Lebanon's Bekaa Valley or around Jerusalem continued small-scale vineyards for sacramental and communal use. Some exports reached European pilgrims. Overall, these wines remained lesser-known internationally but kept ancient traditions alive.

18.7 The New World (Colonial) Regions

18.7.1 Spanish Colonies in the Americas

Mexico, Peru, Chile, Argentina: As discussed in previous chapters, Spanish missionaries introduced the Mission grape (Listán Prieto) for sacramental wine. Over centuries, local clones adapted. By the early 19th century, these regions produced enough wine for domestic use, but official Spanish policies long restricted large-scale exports.

Regional Identities: Peru developed Pisco from grapes; Chile's Central Valley thrived with vineyard expansions; Argentina harnessed the Andean irrigation near Mendoza. Although overshadowed by Europe in fame, these areas laid the groundwork for future wine industries. Independence in the early 19th century gradually opened more opportunities for growth.

18.7.2 Portuguese Brazil

Brazil's tropical or subtropical climate hindered classic European wine grapes. Early attempts near Rio de Janeiro or in the northeast generally failed. Only in southern states—like Rio Grande do Sul—did mild climates permit some success. However, before the late 19th century, Brazilian wine remained minimal and mostly local.

18.7.3 North America

California: Under Spanish and Mexican rule, missions in California planted the Mission grape. By the early 1800s, small-scale wineries existed around missions like San Gabriel or San Diego. True commercial success awaited the mid-19th century (the Gold Rush era), beyond our scope, but seeds of a regional identity were visible.

Other Colonies: The British colonies on the East Coast faced climate and disease obstacles. Consequently, they mostly relied on imported wines from Madeira, Port, or Bordeaux. Hybrid grape experiments took hold in places like Ohio only in the early-to-mid 19th century, with modest local impact at best.

18.8 Key Factors Shaping Regional Development

18.8.1 Climate and Geography

From Bordeaux's maritime influence to the high-altitude deserts of Mendoza, climate strongly dictated which vines thrived. Regions with mild winters and warm summers typically produced consistent yields. Areas with more extreme conditions developed specialized grapes or styles (e.g., sweet, fortified).

18.8.2 Political Control and Trade

Empires, monarchs, and colonial powers decided which wines could be exported, taxed, or restricted. For instance, Britain's conflicts with France spurred the rise of Port. Spanish regulations limited American colonial wine exports, while the Catholic Church's needs for sacramental wine supported monastery-run vineyards.

18.8.3 Cultural and Religious Influences

Monastic orders in Europe, Islamic law in Ottoman territories, or Catholic missions in the Americas each shaped how vineyards were planted and managed. Local customs, from the Greek islands to China's frontier outposts, determined consumption and trade patterns. Over time, alliances (e.g., the Methuen Treaty between Portugal and England) propelled certain regions to renown.

18.9 Challenges and Shifts Toward the 19th Century

18.9.1 War and Instability

The Napoleonic Wars upended wine commerce in Europe. South American revolutions ended Spanish control, opening new local markets. Political upheavals sometimes destroyed vineyards or forced swift changes in production. Nevertheless, the innate demand for wine endured, spurring regions to rebuild once stability returned.

18.9.2 Disease Threats

Before the full onset of phylloxera in the late 19th century, powdery mildew and other fungal issues still caused regional declines. Yet these diseases also prompted early collaboration among vineyard owners, fostering research and solutions that laid the groundwork for the intense efforts that would come with phylloxera's arrival.

18.9.3 Emerging Technologies

As roads and canals improved, trade accelerated. The earliest rail lines in places like Britain and France (1830s–1840s) promised faster shipping, connecting inland vineyards to coastal ports. Glass bottle production advanced, enabling long-distance transport of sealed wines. While pre-modern in scale, these innovations hinted at a more interconnected wine market on the horizon.

CHAPTER 19

Growing Wine Knowledge and Techniques

19.1 Introduction

From the first accidental discoveries of fermentation thousands of years ago to the more systematic approaches emerging in the 18th and 19th centuries, people have slowly uncovered the secrets of making and preserving wine. Early methods involved guesswork and tradition, passed on through families or monastic orders. Over time, better understanding of fermentation, vineyard management, and storage shaped more reliable and diverse wine styles.

In this chapter, we look at how wine knowledge and techniques grew, focusing on the period before modern scientific breakthroughs. We will explore ancient practices that guided Greek and Roman vintners, medieval monastic contributions, the influence of Renaissance curiosity, and the slow but steady adoption of experimental methods in the 18th and early 19th centuries. Along the way, we will see how certain key concepts—like sanitation, temperature control, and blending—evolved, laying the groundwork for the eventual rise of enology (wine science) in later eras.

19.2 Early Approaches to Winemaking

19.2.1 Ancient Accidents and Observations

The earliest wine makers likely relied on pure chance. Grapes left in a container spontaneously fermented due to wild yeast. Once people realized this transformed the juice into an alcoholic beverage with unique flavors, they tried to repeat the process. Early containers—animal skins, clay pots—offered the first "fermentation vessels." Over centuries, communities learned that certain vessels (like sealed pottery jars) worked better at keeping air out.

Cultures in the Caucasus region, Mesopotamia, and Egypt refined basic techniques. They recognized the importance of ripe grapes (for higher sugar) and cooler storage areas. Yet the process remained mysterious. People attributed fermentation's bubbles and foam to divine forces. In Egypt, scribes recorded minimal notes about harvest times and vineyard yields, but they did not fully understand yeast or microbial action. Still, these civilizations formed the foundational techniques—crushing grapes, pressing, storing, and sometimes flavoring with herbs or resins.

19.2.2 Greek Innovations

Ancient Greek texts introduce some thoughtful steps toward consistent winemaking. Vineyards were carefully chosen on sunny slopes, and harvest timing was noted. Writers like Hesiod offered advice on selecting the right moment for picking grapes to avoid unripe or rotten fruit. Greeks also recognized that diluting wine with water moderated its strength and extended the supply.

Greek pottery, such as the **pithos** (large storage jar) and **amphora** (transport vessel), helped control temperature. Many Greek amphorae were lined with pitch or resin to prevent spoilage, though this also imparted distinct flavors. Over time, certain areas specialized in sweet or spiced wines. While Greek authors seldom used the word "technique," their works, combined with archaeological finds, show that structured vineyard care and repeated fermentation practices became more deliberate than in earlier eras.

19.2.3 Roman Refinements

Romans inherited Greek knowledge and pushed it further. Authors like Cato, Varro, and Columella wrote treatises on agriculture, describing vineyard layout, pruning methods, grape crushing, and fermentation in some detail. For example, Columella's works mention controlling the ratio of must (grape juice) to grape skins for certain styles, or using sulfured amphorae to improve shelf life—a technique that vaguely mirrored modern use of sulfur dioxide as an anti-spoilage agent.

Romans also recognized the effect of oak casks—especially from certain forests, though widespread use of wooden barrels was more associated with Gallic or Celtic methods. While amphorae remained common for shipping, some Roman outposts began using wooden barrels to store and transport wine inland. With an extensive empire, the Romans tested grapes in varied climates, developing local solutions to pests, soil differences, or temperature extremes. These trial-and-error experiences paved the way for medieval monastic traditions.

19.3 Medieval Monastic Contributions

19.3.1 Preservation of Techniques

With the collapse of the Western Roman Empire, much agricultural knowledge might have been lost had monasteries not preserved it. Monks needed wine for the Eucharist. They studied surviving Roman texts, maintaining vineyard practices and sometimes improving them. Regions like Burgundy, the Rhine Valley, and parts of Italy served as key centers of continuity.

Monasteries meticulously documented vineyard yields, weather patterns, and pressing methods in their account books. Over generations, they noted which plots produced superior wine and experimented with planting strategies—like spacing vines or training them on stakes for better sun exposure. While these notes did not form a unified scientific text, they offered incremental improvements.

19.3.2 Soil Observation and Terroir

Medieval monks in Burgundy famously observed that certain clos (walled vineyards) or hillside parcels made better wine. They might test different pruning dates or discover the best harvest moment by tasting grapes for sweetness. These repeated observations, year after year, became a rudimentary form of terroir science, linking land, climate, and variety.

Similar patterns occurred along the Rhine, where monastic orders recognized that the steep slate slopes produced refined, aromatic white wines. Their careful vineyard records laid a foundation for the idea that local conditions shaped wine character—though formal chemical analysis did not yet exist.

19.3.3 Innovations in Cellar Management

Monastic cellars introduced consistent temperature controls by situating barrels underground or partly buried. This kept wine cool, slowing spoilage. Wooden barrels replaced some older clay vessels, offering easier handling in large monastic estates. Trial and error revealed that periodic racking (transferring wine off its sediment) improved clarity and flavor.

To address spoilage, some monks used fumigation—burning small sulfur wicks inside empty barrels. This practice (echoing Roman hints) reduced bacterial or fungal contamination. Though they lacked microbiological explanations, monks recognized that sulfur prevented wine from turning to vinegar.

19.4 Renaissance Curiosity and Early Scientific Glimpses

19.4.1 Rediscovery of Classical Texts

The Renaissance saw scholars rediscover works by ancient Roman authors like Columella, reintroducing those agricultural insights to a new generation. Wealthy landowners or courts tried to replicate Roman vineyard setups, sometimes with mixed success. Meanwhile, trade expansions made people more aware of different regional wine styles—spurring interest in how wine was made in far-flung places.

The printing press (15th century) allowed limited circulation of agricultural manuals. Italian, French, and German authors produced treatises on horticulture, occasionally including sections on grape growing and winemaking. Yet these texts remained more descriptive than truly scientific. They described steps to avoid spoilage or manage fermentation but lacked an understanding of yeasts or precise chemical processes.

19.4.2 Experimental Landowners

Some Renaissance princes or aristocrats became "gentleman farmers," launching experimental vineyards. They might import vines from other regions to test adaptability. For instance, a Tuscan noble might try Greek vines on his estate, or a French lord might attempt Spanish grapes. Observing successes or failures broadened knowledge about variety choices, pruning methods, and microclimates.

Alchemists occasionally studied wine for potential medicinal or chemical properties, noting how alcohol could dissolve substances. While alchemy often chased elusive goals (like turning lead into gold), the side effect was collecting data on distillation and fermentation byproducts. This later influenced brandy-making in regions like Cognac or Armagnac, bridging wine and distilled spirits.

19.4.3 The Birth of "Controlled" Fermentation—In Theory

By the late Renaissance, some authors speculated that wine's fermentation required living agents—though they lacked proof. They noted that if a batch was sealed too soon, it tasted strange (often stuck fermentation). If it was left too open, it might sour (vinegar). They recommended moderate ventilation or stirring to manage fermentation speed. These practices were still guesswork but indicated a growing awareness that conditions like temperature and oxygen exposure mattered for quality.

19.5 17th–18th Centuries: Gradual Advances

19.5.1 Bottling and Corking

One of the most important developments was the improved glass bottle and cork stopper. By the 17th century, stronger coal-fired glass furnaces in England allowed thicker bottles. Cork, harvested from cork oak trees in southwestern Europe, provided an airtight seal. Wine stored in such bottles could age longer without spoiling.

This change gradually spread across Europe in the 18th century, revolutionizing how wine was preserved and traded. People realized that certain wines (like Bordeaux reds or Champagne) improved with bottle aging, while others were best consumed young. The idea of a "vintage" took hold, as bottling from a particular harvest year allowed flavor distinctions to develop over time.

19.5.2 Clarification and Fining

Wine clarity was associated with quality. Producers experimented with methods like egg-white fining, adding beaten egg whites to barrels so that proteins would bind with suspended particles and fall to the bottom. This approach might have begun in Spain or Portugal for Sherry and Port, then spread to France and beyond. While the underlying chemistry was still unexplained, trial-and-error showed that fining improved appearance and sometimes softened astringent tannins.

Other fining agents included isinglass (from fish bladders) or dried blood (in some older practices), though the latter was less common by the 18th century. Merchant houses looking to ship bright, clear wines used these techniques to impress buyers. This step contributed to a more polished product, especially for foreign markets.

19.5.3 Blending and House Styles

In regions like Bordeaux, Sherry, or Port, producers increasingly saw blending as an art. They combined wines from different vineyards, or even different years, to achieve a consistent house style. For Sherry, the solera system was an advanced form of blending, where fractional amounts of older wine were mixed with younger wine in a tiered arrangement. Although each region had distinct practices, the principle of mixing wines to balance flavors and ensure reliability became more deliberate.

As large merchant houses formed (particularly in Britain, Portugal, and France), they employed cellar masters who specialized in tasting and blending. These experts recognized nuances in barrel samples, adjusting final blends for uniformity. Over time, brand recognition arose, even if formal labeling was not universal. Customers could request a merchant's wine by name, trusting it would taste similar each time.

19.6 Early 19th Century: Seeds of Enological Science

19.6.1 The Influence of Chemistry

Though still in its infancy, chemistry in the late 18th and early 19th century offered glimpses into fermentation's secrets. Scientists like Antoine Lavoisier studied gases and combustion, while others dabbled in identifying alcohol as a separate component of wine. Some landowners kept amateur chemistry labs, measuring sugar content by crude means or observing how temperature shifts affected fermentation speed.

In France, organizations like the **Académie d'Agriculture** occasionally published papers on vineyard diseases or beneficial treatments. The knowledge was patchy and lacked a unifying theory of microbes. But the idea that wine quality involved chemical transformations was taking root, steering away from purely mystical explanations.

19.6.2 Vine Grafting Experiments

Before phylloxera's full outbreak, some agronomists toyed with grafting vines to help them thrive in challenging soils or climates. Rarely, they used American vine cuttings, noticing their vigor. However, the widespread solution of grafting to combat phylloxera came only in the mid-to-late 19th century (as noted in Chapter 14). Still, these early attempts demonstrated an emerging spirit of practical experimentation.

19.6.3 Documentation of Best Practices

Wine merchants and landowners increasingly recorded harvest dates, fermentation conditions, and cellar temperatures. Some used simple thermometers to track degrees of heat during fermentation. A few published guides for fellow growers, detailing how to select healthy grapes, remove rotten ones, or manage maceration times for deeper color in red wines.

Notably, some French treatises from the 1820s–1840s mention methods to avoid oxidation—racking wine off the lees and transferring it into clean barrels under protective coverings (burning sulfur). Although these were not foolproof, they showed a more systematic approach to preventing spoilage. Over decades, such incremental knowledge built the framework for more advanced enology that would come in the late 19th century.

19.7 Regional Case Studies of Technical Growth

19.7.1 Bordeaux's Merchant Influence

Bordeaux's large-scale trade to Britain and Northern Europe spurred continuing improvements in vineyard care. Merchants demanded stable wines that could travel. Estates like Château Haut-Brion or others in the Médoc (prior to the 1855 Classification) tweaked fermentation times, used selective picking, and sometimes aged wines longer in barrels to ensure consistent results. The pressure of commerce and competition sharpened their technical edge, though fully modern methods still lay ahead.

19.7.2 Champagne's Sparkle

Champagne's method for producing sparkling wine was refined in the 18th and early 19th centuries. Early adopters faced exploding bottles due to uncontrolled secondary fermentation pressure. Gradually, winemakers learned to use thicker glass, measure sugar content, and develop "riddling" techniques (rotating bottles to consolidate sediment near the cork). Madame Clicquot is credited with pioneering riddling racks in the early 19th century. By perfecting these steps, the region gained an innovative reputation.

19.7.3 Douro Valley and Sherry Triangles

In the Douro (Portugal) and Jerez (Spain), the concept of fortification advanced. Producers discovered that timing the addition of grape spirit during fermentation controlled sweetness. They also realized that partial oxidation in barrels could create complex flavors. The British-Portuguese trade, plus local Spanish traditions, encouraged methodical aging processes, leading to consistent "house styles" for Port and Sherry. This focus on blending and cask management became a model for other regions seeking stable exports.

19.8 Knowledge Transfer and Education

19.8.1 Agricultural Societies

By the early 19th century, some European regions boasted agricultural societies that met to discuss crop yields, pests, or new tools. While these societies covered more than just vines, many had subgroups focusing on wine. Annual or periodic gatherings let vineyard owners exchange successes and failures, forging a rudimentary peer network.

Publications from these societies sometimes reached beyond local borders, spreading new ideas—like improved pruning patterns or anti-fungal washes. Though the modern idea of "wine science conferences" did not exist, these forums were stepping stones to more organized research.

19.8.2 Apprenticeships and Family Transmission

Despite the emergence of written guides, most practical wine knowledge still passed from generation to generation within families or through apprentices. A young vintner learned to taste grape ripeness, gauge fermentation progress, and manage cellars by working closely with elders who had absorbed the same knowledge from their predecessors. This hands-on tradition gave each region a distinctive style shaped by local wisdom, but it also sometimes slowed the spread of new methods if families were resistant to change.

19.8.3 Influence of Monastic and Ecclesiastical Schools

In parts of Germany, Austria, and France, church-linked schools occasionally taught basic viticulture. These institutions might instruct novices in orchard management, including vines, focusing on practical tasks like grafting or orchard sanitation. Over time, some lay institutions followed suit, offering vineyard courses at agricultural academies. By the 19th century, a handful of specialized schools were budding, though still rare.

19.9 The State of Wine Knowledge Before Modern Times

19.9.1 Strengths and Limitations

By the mid-19th century, many wine regions had become adept at controlling aspects of production—site selection, pruning, fermentation vessels, racking, aging in barrels or bottles. Traders and nobles demanded consistent quality, fueling incremental innovations. Yet fundamental scientific concepts—like the role of yeast or the microbial nature of spoilage—remained largely unknown. Much was still guesswork and custom, leading to frequent spoilage or inconsistent vintages.

19.9.2 Variation and Cultural Diversity

Local traditions stayed strong. Bordeaux's method for red blends differed from Piedmont's extended maceration with Nebbiolo, or from the solera aging of Sherry. Each region, shaped by environment and history, developed specialized techniques that travelers sometimes described with wonder. This diversity was both a challenge and a cultural treasure: no single approach dominated, allowing for a variety of styles well before standardization.

19.9.3 Challenges Looming on the Horizon

Even as knowledge advanced, bigger trials awaited: phylloxera (as discussed), global trade expansions, and political changes that would reorder markets. The more systematic science of fermentation, championed by figures like Louis Pasteur (late 19th century), had yet to emerge. So, while progress was real, the world of pre-modern wine existed in a transitional phase—poised between centuries-old customs and the brink of deeper chemical understanding.

CHAPTER 20

Reflections and the Road to the Early Modern Era

20.1 Introduction

After traversing many centuries—from the first traces of wine in prehistoric vessels to the steady improvements in vineyard and cellar practices by the early 19th century—it is clear that wine is much more than a drink. It is an essential cultural artifact, shaped by geography, politics, religion, art, and commerce. Each chapter in this book has revealed a facet of wine's deep roots, showing how it accompanied humanity's social, economic, and spiritual development.

In this final chapter, we will summarize the major themes, highlight key turning points, and consider how wine's long history sets the stage for what we might call the early modern era. This concluding overview will remind us why wine matters—not just to wine lovers, but to anyone interested in human civilization. We will also note the challenges and legacies inherited by the generations who carried wine into more modern times, while respecting our limit of staying within older historical contexts.

20.2 Major Themes and Timelines

20.2.1 From Accidental Discovery to Organized Production

One consistent thread is how humans moved from stumbling upon fermented grape juice to intentionally cultivating vineyards. This shift required centuries of trial and error—understanding soil types, climates, and the basic need for cleanliness to prevent spoilage.

Early civilizations in the Near East recognized wine's ritual and social value. Greeks refined communal drinking customs (symposia). Romans systematized agricultural practices, building an empire-wide viticultural network.

20.2.2 The Role of Religion

Wine's story is inseparable from faith traditions. Egyptian temple offerings, Mesopotamian libations, and especially the Christian Eucharist anchored wine in religious ceremonies. Monastic orders safeguarded viticulture knowledge through medieval Europe, bridging the fall of Rome to the Renaissance. Judaism's Sabbath and festival rituals likewise preserved wine's symbolic significance. Even in regions with Islamic rule, wine production often continued under certain allowances for non-Muslim or medicinal use, though in smaller scope.

20.2.3 Commerce and Politics

Wine frequently intersected with power and trade. Empires like Rome or maritime republics like Venice exchanged wine across territories. Later, British demand for Bordeaux or Portuguese Port shaped entire regional economies. Political treaties, wars, and alliances either boosted or blocked wine exports. This interplay made wine a valuable commodity that could drive diplomacy—like the Methuen Treaty for Port—or face blockades in times of conflict.

20.2.4 Artistic and Cultural Expressions

Artists, poets, and storytellers have continuously used wine to symbolize joy, love, transformation, and sometimes downfall. From Dionysian cult imagery on Greek vases to Renaissance banquets in grand paintings, wine's cultural footprint enriched artistic heritage. Literature also mirrored society's changing attitudes: comedic caution, romantic inspiration, or moral warnings. This depth of representation underlines wine's central place in human imagination and identity.

20.3 Key Turning Points

20.3.1 Spread of Wine in the Ancient World

The diffusion from the Near East to Egypt, Mesopotamia, Greece, and Rome was a critical expansion phase. As each civilization adopted wine, it personalized the beverage—shifting from a local curiosity to a pan-Mediterranean staple by classical times. This set the foundation for wine to become integral to Western civilization.

20.3.2 Medieval Preservation

After Rome's fall, monastic communities preserved both the technique of viticulture and the notion of wine's religious significance. This era shaped Europe's vineyard distribution, as monastic orders cleared land, identified prime plots, and documented repeated vintage variations.

20.3.3 The Age of Exploration

The 15th–17th centuries saw wine carried overseas by European explorers and colonists. Spanish missions in the Americas, Portuguese footholds in Africa and Asia, and subsequent colonial expansions transplanted Old World grapes into new soils. Although restricted by imperial policies at first, these plantings seeded future global wine industries.

20.3.4 17th–18th Century Commerce and Techniques

The emergence of major trading nations—England, the Netherlands, France, Spain, and Portugal—fostered new markets. Fortified wines like Port and Sherry, along with the early sparkling experiments in Champagne, diversified styles. The adoption of glass bottles and corks improved storage and aging, gradually unveiling the nuances of vintage variation and long-term refinement.

20.3.5 Early 19th Century Knowledge Gains

Rudimentary science, better documentation, and the impetus of international trade propelled further refinements. While still lacking microbial insights, wine producers recognized the value of controlling fermentation temperature, limiting oxidation, and employing fining techniques. Merchant demands for stable, transportable wines spurred more consistent approaches, though major scientific breakthroughs awaited the late 19th century.

20.4 Challenges and Transformations at the Threshold of Modernity

20.4.1 The Phylloxera Crisis (Late 19th Century)

As detailed earlier, phylloxera ravaged Europe's vineyards from the 1860s onward, compelling replanting with American rootstocks. This catastrophe introduced radical changes, including standardized rootstock usage, more uniform vineyard layouts, and advanced research in ampelography. Though phylloxera's main devastation falls slightly beyond the "early 19th century," it marks a turning point that reshaped global viticulture.

20.4.2 Industrial Age Impact

Even before the fully modern era, developments in transport—steamships, railways—began connecting wine regions to distant markets. Bulk wine shipments grew, and urban populations demanded consistent supplies. Some regions mechanized aspects of vineyard work, though widespread mechanization would only come later. Still, these shifts signaled the end of an epoch where wine production was almost entirely manual and locally oriented.

20.4.3 Emergence of Scientific Enology

By the mid-to-late 19th century, scientists like Louis Pasteur (active in the 1850s–1860s) studied fermentation, clarifying yeast's role. Though Pasteur's deeper contributions belong to more modern times, their seeds appeared in the early 19th century's growing curiosity about chemical transformations. This paved the way for enology as a separate field, with dedicated laboratories, formal training, and advanced disease management.

20.5 Wine's Enduring Social and Cultural Functions

20.5.1 Community and Celebration

Historically, wine has served as a communal bond in many societies. Festivals, weddings, harvest gatherings, and religious ceremonies revolve around shared cups. This tradition transcended time, whether in ancient Mesopotamian temples or medieval European taverns. In each context, wine provided not just flavor, but a sense of unity and identity.

20.5.2 Symbolic and Spiritual Resonance

From Dionysus and Bacchus to the Christian Eucharist, wine carried deep symbolic weight. It represented transformation, celebration, sacrifice, or divine presence. Artistic and literary works spanning millennia captured these layers, ensuring wine's place in the spiritual and creative realm.

20.5.3 Health and Medicine

Even before modern science, wine was seen as a remedy or tonic in many cultures. Ancient Egyptian, Greek, and Roman texts mention wine-based medicines. Medieval monasteries used wine in herbal infusions. While some claims were exaggerated, many recognized that moderate wine consumption could be safer than unsanitized water. By the early 19th century, doctors still debated wine's medicinal role, but no one doubted its widespread acceptance as a daily beverage in certain regions.

20.6 Legacies for the Future

20.6.1 Preservation of Regional Character

Each major wine region—Bordeaux, Burgundy, Champagne, Douro, Sherry, Rhine, Tokaj, Chianti, and countless others—carried forward a proud local identity by 1850. Their distinct grapes and methods were anchored in centuries of tradition, ensuring that even as global challenges arose (like phylloxera), they would strive to preserve uniqueness.

20.6.2 The Spread of Vines Worldwide

European colonial ventures introduced grapes to the Americas, Africa, and parts of Asia, often via missionary work. Though restricted by climate or politics, these plantings laid seeds for future wine industries. By the early 19th century, local production in places like Chile, Argentina, or California was still small, but the foundation was set. Decades or centuries later, these New World regions would blossom into global wine contenders, thanks to inherited Old World techniques.

20.6.3 Formation of Early Wine Science

Long before modern enology degrees, the combination of monastic records, merchant blending practices, experimental landowners, and budding scientific interest shaped a knowledge base. This synergy foreshadowed the rise of formal wine institutes, chemical labs, and, eventually, a deeper microbial understanding. The 19th-century leaps in technology and transportation pushed wine from a local craft toward a more standardized global commodity.

20.7 Concluding Reflections

20.7.1 A Journey Across Millennia

Our exploration has traversed prehistoric pottery shards, ancient Egyptian tomb paintings, Greek amphora art, Roman treatises, medieval monastic cellars, Renaissance curiosity, and 18th–19th-century commercial expansions. In each era, wine adapted to new conditions, reflecting both continuity and change. The vine's resilience, paired with human ingenuity, ensured that wine remained a central thread in civilizations across continents.

20.7.2 Why Wine Endures

Wine's durability stems from its dual nature: it is both a utilitarian food product and a symbol-laden cultural artifact. It satisfies thirst and palate while feeding imaginations—art, religion, mythology, and literature all tapped wine's metaphorical power. Its fermentation process evokes transformation, bridging the tangible and the mystical. This unique status has made wine an enduring companion to human history.

20.7.3 On the Threshold of the Modern Age

By the early 19th century—our cutoff for this comprehensive historical overview—wine was poised for even greater developments. Industrialization, phylloxera, expanding international trade, and the forthcoming scientific revolution would drastically reshape vineyards and cellars. But the core legacy of centuries past—local grape varieties, carefully honed regional methods, centuries-old festival traditions—would persist as the soul of wine, even under modern influences.

20.8 What We Can Take Forward

20.8.1 Respect for Heritage

Understanding wine's extensive past fosters gratitude for the labor and creativity of countless generations. Each region's wine is the product of many stories—monks, farmers, explorers, scientists, and artists. Protecting historic vineyards or rare indigenous grapes honors that legacy. Although we do not delve into modern practices here, the principle of safeguarding cultural heritage remains.

20.8.2 Lessons in Adaptation

From ancient clay pots to the wooden barrels of the medieval period, from the partial sealing of amphorae to the precise cork closures, wine has evolved through continuous adaptation. Geography, climate swings, political upheavals—wine culture overcame them all through flexible thinking. This reminds us that resilience and innovation are cornerstones of human endeavors, especially when it comes to agricultural products.

20.8.3 The Interplay of Science and Tradition

Even before formal enology, scientific inklings guided improvements—like controlling fermentation temperature or using sulfur to prevent spoilage. At the same time, deep-rooted traditions and local knowledge proved invaluable. True progress often blended both elements: a respect for time-tested practices with a willingness to experiment. This dual approach shaped wine's historical progression and set the stage for breakthroughs that arrived in the late 19th century and beyond.

20.9 A Final Word on Historical Perspectives

Though wine can be seen simply as a beverage, its journey from antiquity to the threshold of modernity demonstrates a microcosm of human progress—agricultural, social, and intellectual. Emperors and peasants, monks and merchants, artists and farmers all contributed to wine's narrative. War, peace, trade, religion, and science each left their imprint. By studying wine's pre-modern evolution, we gain a lens to view broader human history.

20.10 Chapter and Book Summary

- **Wine as a Cultural Constant**: From prehistoric gatherings to early 19th-century estates, wine bridged daily life, faith, art, and trade.
- **Key Themes**: Religion's role, political influences, artistic representation, and developing techniques all shaped wine's story.
- **Growing Knowledge**: Ancient trial-and-error evolved into monastic records, Renaissance experimentation, and early 19th-century chemistry.
- **Significant Regions**: Bordeaux, Burgundy, Champagne, Rhine, Douro, Sherry, Tokaj, Italy's diverse zones, Eastern Mediterranean, and colonial vineyards all contributed their own methods and identities.
- **Challenges and Shifts**: War, diseases like phylloxera, and industrial developments tested wine culture, pushing it toward modern solutions.
- **Legacy**: Wine remains a testament to human cooperation with nature, resilience under adversity, and the quest to refine taste and technique across centuries.

With this final overview, we conclude *The History of Wine*. We have traversed a vast timeline, revealing how, through countless innovations and challenges, wine has maintained its place at the heart of human culture. Though we end before modern industrial revolutions, the seeds of today's global wine industry were firmly planted in these earlier periods. May this historical journey inspire a deeper appreciation for wine's ancient origins, diverse traditions, and enduring bond with humanity.

Help Us Share Your Thoughts!

Dear reader,

Thank you for spending your time with this book. We hope it brought you enjoyment and a few new ideas to think about. If there was anything that didn't work for you, or if you have suggestions on how we can improve, please let us know at **kontakt@skriuwer.com**. Your feedback means a lot to us and helps us make our books even better.

If you enjoyed this book, we would be very grateful if you left a review on the site where you purchased it. Your review not only helps other readers find our books, but also encourages us to keep creating more stories and materials that you'll love.

By choosing Skriuwer, you're also supporting **Frisian**—a minority language mainly spoken in the northern Netherlands. Although **Frisian** has a rich history, the number of speakers is shrinking, and it's at risk of dying out. Your purchase helps fund resources to preserve and promote this language, such as educational programs and learning tools. If you'd like to learn more about Frisian or even start learning it yourself, please visit **www.learnfrisian.com**.

Thank you for being part of our community. We look forward to sharing more books with you in the future.

Warm regards,
The Skriuwer Team

www.ingramcontent.com/pod-product-compliance
Lightning Source LLC
LaVergne TN
LVHW012042070526
838202LV00056B/5565